Therapy and the Arts

THERAPY and the ARTS

Tools of Consciousness

Edited by
Walt Anderson

HARPER COLOPHON BOOKS
Harper & Row, Publishers
New York, Hagerstown, San Francisco, London

Grateful acknowledgment is hereby made for permission to reprint the following:

From *Arrow in the Blue* by Arthur Koestler. © Arthur Koestler 1952, 1969. Reprinted by permission of Macmillan Publishing Co., Inc.

From "Dream Deferred" by Langston Hughes. Copyright 1951 by Langston Hughes. Reprinted from *The Panther and the Lash: Poems of Our Times* by permission of Alfred A. Knopf, Inc.

From *Listening with the Third Ear: The Inner Experience of a Psychoanalyst* by Theodor Reik. Copyright 1948 by Theodor Reik, copyright renewed 1976 by Arthur Reik. Reprinted by permission of Farrar, Straus & Giroux, Inc.

"Poem Number 8" ("In Golden Gate Park that day"), Lawrence Ferlinghetti, *A Coney Island of the Mind.* Copyright © 1958 by Lawrence Ferlinghetti. Reprinted by permission of New Directions Publishing Corporation.

From "You, Doctor Martin" by Anne Sexton. Reprinted from *To Bedlam and Part Way Back* by permission of Houghton Mifflin Company.

Designed by Eve Kirch Callahan

First edition: HARPER COLOPHON BOOKS, 1977

LIBRARY OF CONGRESS CATALOG CARD NUMBER: 75–814

STANDARD BOOK NUMBER: 06–090429–1

77 78 79 80 5 4 3 2 1

Contents

Introduction

We are a people much given to compartmentalized thinking; it makes life orderly and sets the modern mind at rest to know that a doctor is a person who does one thing, an artist a person who does something else; that colleges naturally have separate departments of art, drama, English, and psychology; that people who want to be entertained go to the movies, people who are suffering severe emotional stress go to the therapists, and people who are in search of mystical enlightenment go to gurus and Zen masters.

Fortunately, the compartmentalization process has never entirely succeeded. It has, it is true, triumphed over the minds of administrators and bureaucrats; and on paper—look at a college catalogue or an organizational diagram—it seems to be a serene and complete representation of reality. But at the level of human experience things are not so simple; our deepest needs and feelings do not always know how society is organized.

There was a time when the compartments had hardly taken form at all: in ancient Greece the drama was not only expression for playwright and actors, and entertainment for audiences; it was also a religious ceremony, a public festival, a political and social institution, and—as Aristotle knew—a path to personal growth through the catharsis of emotions and the development of insight.

And in our own time a good deal of partition-destroying is going on. Artists and psychotherapists keep returning to the roots of the experiences they deal with, and borrowing from one another as they go: therapists use painting, sculpture, poetry, and a variety of other techniques to help their clients open new channels of self-expression; modern artists and dramatists, similarly, strive not merely to entertain or educate audiences, but to transform consciousness.

Actually, the histories of modern psychotherapy and modern art are closely interwoven. J. L. Moreno, inventor of the oldest of the art therapies, psychodrama, had previously been involved with the direction of Vienna's *Stegreiftheater* (spontaneity theater), one of the first improvisational theater groups. Isadora Duncan, who in this century laid the foundations of modern creative dance, also contributed to the discovery of dance as a way that severely disturbed people could communicate to others and participate in a group activity. Dance therapists, as well as artists, acknowledge the debt to her.

In this volume I want to make clear the natural similarities between art and therapy: by stressing that these two lines of human activity flow out of similar—if not identical—sets of human aspirations, it will be easier to show why therapy and the arts are again drawing closer together. Use of the arts in therapy is not a gimmick; it is a natural and effective pipeline to rich sources of feeling and meaning. Arts and therapy are logically related enterprises: they are tools of consciousness, paths of development of the human mind.

And so, although I do not intend to overlook the clinical and institutional uses of art in therapy—applications with disturbed children, inmates of mental institutions, the physically handicapped, drug addicts—I want to make it clear that the whole movement is now advancing along a much broader front.

The art therapies are proving to be particularly congenial to psychologists who identify themselves with "third force," or humanistic, psychology, with growth centers, the human potential movement, the consciousness revolution. Part of what humanistic psychology is all about is a rejection of the preoccupation with mental illness that is common to Freudian and behaviorist psychologies—their attachment to the "medical model," in which therapy is seen as the "cure" of an identifiable "sickness." The weakness in these older psychologies, argue the humanists, is that, for one thing, they have neglected to form any conception of what real health, true optimum human development, could be. The best they had (as Abraham Maslow put it) was a concept of a normal, well-adjusted person without problems, a most doubtful model of human possibilities. Another weakness—and here the case has been made most forcefully by such writers as R. D. Laing and Thomas Szasz—is that the very existence of such a thing as mental illness is an issue that can be disputed on a wide variety of moral, scientific, legal, and medical grounds and is not a matter to be accepted with as much ease and certainty as the established psychiatric profession and allied mental-health bureaucracy seem to believe. The kinds of behaviors so readily labeled "schizophrenic," Laing argues, are scarcely understood at all in any objective medical sense, and the states we call "mad" represent complex human efforts to survive, to relate, to perceive reality, to explore life—they are efforts that must be regarded with respect, compassion, and perhaps even a touch of awe. They are not merely to be administered *to* by wise doctors and sane society, but also to be learned *from*.

Now, all these psychological issues have much to do with how one uses art. If therapy is regarded as an activity covering a vast range of human development—not merely making the sick healthy but also making the healthy healthier, finding and opening new doors to the highest reaches of personal potential— then the use of the arts, humanity's oldest body of resources for expression and self-realization, has a natural place. It is equally reasonable that when we are dealing with the "mentally ill," we would wish to provide them the widest possible range of tools for working through their experiences. And furthermore, if we are ready to accept the possibility that those experiences contain insights that would be of meaning and value to us all, we want to establish paths of communication. We can see both the insane and the sane in the same way Antonin Artaud saw the participants in true drama, as "victims burnt at the stake, signaling through the flames."[1]

Art and therapy are both involved with the expansion of consciousness; often this is stated as an attempt to bring about a productive integration of the conscious and the unconscious. Arthur Koestler describes it as a sequence: a regression (into the

---

1. Antonin Artaud, *The Theater and Its Double,* trans. Mary Caroline Richards (New York: Grove Press, 1958) , p. 13.

primitive, the irrational, the infantile, or the instinctual) is followed by a leap forward, a new and creative organization of the
individual within the environment.

Sidney Jourard's definition of growth runs closely parallel to
this: "Growth," said Jourard, "is the dis-integration of one way
of experiencing the world, followed by a re-organization of this
experience, a reorganization that includes the new disclosures
of the world. The disorganization, or even shattering, of one way
to experience the world, is brought on by new disclosures . . .
disclosures that were always being transmitted, but were usually
ignored."[2]

These disintegrative crises are a common part of human experience. In science, for example, Thomas Kuhn's *The Structure
of Scientific Revolutions* offered a radical new view of the nature
of scientific discovery, contradicting the conventional image of
science as a steady development of theory through the piecemeal
addition of data. According to Kuhn, theories become dogma,
and new data are determinedly ignored until they become so
intrusive that some pioneer forms them into an entirely new
paradigm, which then totally shatters the old one. Following
this, there is a period of chaos and uncertainty, and then a leap
forward.

But the scientist—at least a revolutionary paradigm builder
such as Copernicus, Darwin, or Einstein—possesses rare tools of
consciousness: an openness to new data (which is itself evidence
of a high order of personal development, an enhanced ability to
trust experience) combined with an intellectual ability to create
a new paradigm, to bring order out of what had once been chaos.

Most of us are less forunate: our tools for passing through
the periodic disintegrations and reintegrations of growth and
self-actualization are less highly developed. For virtually all
civilized human beings, the everyday procedure for avoiding
the pain and confusion of disintegration is the same as that of
the gentlemen who refused to look through Galileo's telescope:
we shut out experience. We shut out a good portion of our sense
perceptions, our emotions, our needs and feelings, and operate

2. Sidney M. Jourard, "Growing Awareness and the Awareness of Growth,"
in *Ways of Growth,* ed. Herbert A. Otto and John Mann (New York: The
Viking Press, 1968), p. 2.

at some tolerably comfortable level of unawareness. And (as Freud described the mechanism of repression) we also shut out the fact that we are shutting out. But for some people, periodically or continually, the shutting-out process fails to function, the task is too great: the raw data of experience flood into awareness, and the individual experiences the kind of disintegration we call psychosis. Classical psychoanalysis, recognizing this, described neurosis as a defense against psychosis. Gestalt therapy, stating the matter somewhat differently, describes the avoidance of awareness as the way people protect themselves from the painful and fearful experiences that lead to new integration and personal growth. In Gestalt theory—and this puts the case in a fairly representative way for humanistic psychology in general—the goal of therapy is a recovery of awareness, a reawakening to the senses, a reowning of one's life experience.

It has been apparent throughout the history of psychiatry that there is some natural connection between the process of artistic creation and the process of psychotherapy. Freud was interested in the lives of creative artists and wrote psychological studies of Dostoevsky and Leonardo da Vinci; Ernest Jones launched a whole new school of Shakespearean interpretation with his *Hamlet and Oedipus.* Those works took art to be a window into the subconscious; the artist's creations were seen as disguised expressions of neurosis, which could be analyzed for general insights. Artistic expression was considered to be a form of sublimation, of channeling neurotic drives into socially acceptable forms.

Sublimation was a desirable end goal of Freudian therapy, but "acting out" of inner conflicts was not. The psychoanalyst did indeed recognize the need to get in touch with the subconscious, but the only acceptable method was the free-association monologue in which the patient verbally communicated dreams and memories to the analyst; an insight into the source of emotions was the goal, but the process itself was an intellectual and scrupulously unemotional one.

The prohibition against acting out was the point of departure for psychodrama. J. L. Moreno not only permitted acting out but encouraged it, made it the keystone of his therapy and, incidentally, of his own personal life.

"I wanted to show," Moreno has written of himself, "that here is a man who has all the signs of paranoia and megalomania, exhibitionism and social maladjustment, and who can still be fairly well controlled and healthy, and indeed, of apparently greater productivity by acting them out than if he would have tried to constrain and resolve his symptoms—the living antithesis of psychoanalysis. . . ."[3]

Moreno made spontaneity and creativity the key values of his therapy. The therapeutic process itself is a Dionysian one, a free releasing of expression: dreams, fantasies, daydreams of revenge, demands for love and attention—all can be acted out in the freewheeling psychodramatic session; nothing has to be held back. Psychodrama operates on the belief that repressing socially unacceptable feelings and fantasies is not only a huge drain on human energies but also, paradoxically, a sure way of keeping the feelings and fantasies alive: to act them out is to confront the ghost in broad daylight. The subject of psychodrama finds that the hidden angers that seemed to be of huge and murderous dimensions most often have a human size, and the group process often reveals that many feelings are more "normal" than individuals had suspected.

The point of using spontaneity and creativity in therapy is to enable the individual to become more spontaneous and creative in daily life. Creativity—the ability to deal adequately with a new situation or to deal innovatively with an old one—is seen as the very essence of mental health.

Thus psychodrama, like theatrical drama, follows Koestler's pattern: it is a journey into the depths, into the dark places of the human psyche, bringing what is found there out into view, to be confronted and dealt with, while protagonist (the term for patient in psychodrama) and audience experience emotional catharsis and develop new insight—regression, followed by a leap forward.

And the leap forward, in psychodrama and all the other expressive therapies, is more than an adjustment to society, more than the resigned acceptance of a lifelong reining in of the in-

3. Jacob L. Moreno, *Who Shall Survive?* (Beacon, N.Y.: Beacon House, 1953), p. xix.

stincts that Freud saw as the goal of therapy. Consider the difference between Freud's statement to a patient that "much will be gained if we succeed in transforming your hysterical misery into common unhappiness"[4] and Fritz Perls's exuberant description of the goal of Gestalt therapy: "The previously robotized corpses begin to return to life, gaining substance and beginning the dance of abandonment and self-fulfillment; the paper people are turning into real people."[5]

Obviously we are dealing with a different system of values: adjustment is not the goal, and the primitive needs and drives of the human organism are not the enemy. The enemy, rather, is dehumanization: the desensitizing effect of repression, regimented education, technocracy, bureaucracy—the vast alliance of forces that trim and shape the complex and enormously vital human organism down to size to fit a neat, plastic, productive social role. The object, then, is to recover the total person: to develop anew the lost capacities for feeling, spontaneity, expression; to reopen the blocked channels to the childlike and the primitive, the hidden sources of myth and fantasy.

This does not mean, as critics of the expressive growth therapies seem to believe, that regression is the only goal, that any modern civilized human being is expected to become a child or a savage again. The goal is to recover and reintegrate. It is true that much of what has been traditionally considered civilized is rejected, but this comes from the belief that the whole and natural human being possesses a natural capacity for civilized behavior. Thus Theodore Roszak says of Gestalt that it is "one of the few schools of psychiatry that has been prepared to set society at large into the therapeutic scales and to find the way of the world wanting, a mad attack upon human potentialities. Gestalt holds out for the inherent sociability of the whole human being, including his sexual and even his aggressive needs."[6] The same vision of the human potential for a harmonization of

4. Sigmund Freud and Josef Breuer, *Studies on Hysteria*, trans. James Strachey (London: The Hogarth Press, 1955), p. 305.

5. Frederick S. Perls, "Workshop vs. Individual Therapy," paper delivered to the American Psychological Association, New York, September 1966.

6. Theodore Roszak, "Counter Culture IV: The Future as Community," *The Nation*, April 15, 1968, p. 502.

spontaneity with sociability is reflected in Maslow's work with superior, self-actualized people. He found his subjects to be both "good and lusty animals, hearty in their appetites and enjoying themselves without regret or shame or apology"[7] and also more ethical and socially responsible, possessing a more democratic character structure and a more highly devolped sense of membership in the human species. The revolutionary message is clear: the social order does not rest upon repression after all. "It is spontaneity which produces order," says Moreno, "not the laws which are themselves an artefact of a spontaneous order."[8]

Thus we find that the course on which we embark in search of new ways to develop consciousness, to release the human potential for growth, is not only a matter of art and therapy but also of politics: once you have seriously begun to consider the possibility that the adjustment of the individual to the social order is not necessarily any improvement in his or her mental health, then you must logically begin to consider the possibility that it is the social order that must adjust, perhaps change radically in order to facilitate the free development of human beings.

And we must stretch the boundaries still further, because it is also a matter of religion. Traditionally the creative spirit, God, has been thought of as a remote and separate being, who in the unimaginably distant past made the universe and the world and the human race. Even the concept of evolution, offering a doctrine of creation more compatible with the modern scientific *Zeitgeist*, has had a kind of formidable objectivity to it, has seemed to be more a cold set of universal laws than anything having to do with the subjective experience of individuals.

But the spirit of the human potential movement, the "consciousness revolution" as it is sometimes called, tends toward a more subjective and personal view of evolution: it says, in effect, that the universe is being created here and now in the awareness of every living individual, and that evolution—the nature of the human species—is a matter of conscious responsi-

7. A. H. Maslow, "Self-Actualization: A Study in Psychological Health," in *The World of Psychology*, ed. G. B. Levitas (New York: George Braziller, 1963), vol. 2, p. 534.
8. Jacob L. Moreno, *Psychodrama* (Beacon, N.Y.: Beacon House, 1946), vol. 1, p. 9.

bility and choice. Lewis Mumford, one of the greatest American humanists, has argued that this self-creating faculty is the essential, basic characteristic of the human race:

> Every manifestation of human culture, from ritual and speech to costume and social organization, is directed ultimately to the remodelling of the human organism and the expression of the human personality. If it is only now that we belatedly recognize this distinctive feature, it is perhaps because there are widespread indications in contemporary art and politics and technics that man may be on the point of losing it—becoming not a lower animal, but a shapeless, amoeboid nonentity.[9]

The aim and purpose of the human potential movement is to recover and give a contemporary meaning to this deep self-creating spirit, to bring together the arts and sciences into a new and unified vision of what human life is and can become. Within this context, then, we can see that the intermingling of therapy and the arts is far more than a modest interdisciplinary exercise; it is, rather, part of a widespread effort to take a new look at all facets of human experience, to open new paths of evolutionary development. It is work toward the emergence of a new and freer race of beings, more open to their deepest needs and feelings than contemporary overcivilized men and women—able, as Koestler puts it, to regress, and simultaneously able to leap forward, to develop and live in more humane social orders.

The art therapies are concerned with art as subjective experience, as a tool of consciousness, a part of personal life and growth. In many cases they use art in a "curative" way, to release blocked and stunted human capacities for expression and feeling, but this is more than an act of healing: it is also an act of liberation.

9. Lewis Mumford, *The Myth of the Machine* (New York: Harcourt, Brace & World, 1967), pp. 8–9.

Creation and Growth

Arthur Koestler

—•—

Regression and Integration

If creativity is a characteristic of the human species, then clearly it must have roots in our biological heritage. Arthur Koestler argues that it does and that both art and therapy grow out of the same primal life processes. He uses the proverb reculer pour mieux sauter—*run back to get a better jump—as a truth revealed in art, scientific discovery, healing, and evolutionary change. Creation, he says, is a form of mutation, and forward leaps are preceded by—in fact launched by— regressions.*

Reculer sans Sauter

Hyper-excited organs or organ-systems tend to get out of control. During the repair of physical injuries, the injured part tends to monopolize the attention of the whole organism; in periods of starvation, the digestive system asserts itself to the detriment of other parts; in rage and panic, the sympathico-adrenal apparatus tyrannizes the whole; and when sex is aroused, reason (as the Austrian proverb has it) "descends into the testes." The over-excited part behaves as if it were in a temporary state of "physi-ological isolation," released from its restraints; it asserts its autonomy and sometimes tends to usurp the functions of the whole.

Analagous situations occur on the cognitive level, where the "hyper-excited part" appears in the guise of the *idée fixe*, or a "closed system" of beliefs. Both the achievements and the aberrations of human thought are to a large extent due to obsessional preoccupations with religious and scientific theories, or political ideologies, more or less closely knitted around some central idea, around a part-truth usurping the role of the whole truth.

An obsessional pre-occupation can force the whole mental organization into its service during the period of incubation, and give birth to a new system of thought. But these are the glorious exceptions; in the vast majority of cases, the "over-valued idea" (to use Kretschmer's term[1]) will become segregated from the rest of the mental field, and assert itself in harmful ways. The results are all too familiar: personalities whose whole outlook is dominated by prejudice and biassed values; the compulsive rituals of neurotics; the devouring obsession of the crank; and so on to the major psychoses in which large chunks of the personality have been "split off" and become permanently isolated from the rest. The intrusion of magic causation; inability to distinguish between fact and fantasy; delusions of grandeur, or persecution by invisible powers, are symptoms of regression to earlier levels, of the de-differentiation of thought-matrices—of *reculer sans sauter*.

Regeneration and Psychotherapy

Less extreme cases are neurotics who react to their traumatic experiences by elaborating defence systems which enable them to find some kind of *modus vivendi* with the world. One may call such behaviour-patterns "faulty integrations"—like the newt's whose forelegs move backwards. Psychotherapy aims at undoing faulty integrations by inducing a temporary regression of the patient to an earlier level, in the hope that he will eventually reintegrate into a more stable pattern. Neuro-surgery, shock-therapy, and related methods aim at releasing philogenetically older centres of the brain from cortical restraints. In a less drastic form, Freudians, Jungians, etc., try to make the patient revert to

1. E. Kretschmer, *The Psychology of Men of Genius* (London: K. Paul, 1931), p. 138.

unconscious and infantile planes of experience, and to regenerate, as it were, into a more or less new-born person.

Thus psychotherapy may be called an experiment in artificially induced regeneration. It relies on the same basic process of *reculer pour mieux satuer*, which we see operating on every level: from the flatworm which replaces a lost head, through the crab which adjusts its gait to the loss of a leg, to the rat which, unable to turn to the right, makes a three-quarter turn to the left. We found the same pattern repeated on the level of human creativity: the scientist, faced by a perplexing situation—Kepler's discrepant eight minutes' arc, Einstein's light-traveller paradox—must plunge into a "dark night of the soul" before he can re-emerge into the light. The history of the sciences and arts is a tale of recurrent crises, of traumatic challenges, which entail a temporary disintegration of the traditional forms of reasoning and perception: a de-differentiation of thought-matrices, a dismantling of its axioms, a new innocence of the eye; followed by the liberation from restraint of creative potentials, and their reintegration in a new synthesis.

There is also a mental equivalent for the less spectacular routine regeneration of tissues, designed to compensate for wear and tear. The analogue process is the maintenance of "mental tissues" exposed to the wear and tear of diurnal stresses, by the regenerative effect of nocturnal regressions to the primitive levels of the dream. Experimental evidence seems to indicate that the restorative powers of sleep are primarily derived from the process of dreaming. Experimental subjects who were woken up each time their EEG waves indicated the onset of dreaming displayed symptoms of fatigue and nervous disorder; long periods of dreamless sleep could not compensate for dream-deprivation. "Man cannot persist long in a conscious state," wrote Goethe, "he must throw himself back into the unconscious, for his root lives there."

These periodic plunges into the unconscious are accompanied by the temporary disintegration of matrices of logical thought. But they also entail a partial loss of identity, a de-differentiation of the personality—as indicated by the remarkable degree of uniformity in the contents of dreams shared by people of very different character, and by the relatedness of these contents to mythological themes and symbols. These shared patterns led Jung to postulate a "collective"—that is, individually undifferentiated—level of the unconscious. On that level, members of the same culture seem to share some degree of psychic equipotentiality expressed in "archetypal symbols." These are supposed to be condensations of basic experiences of the race in the distant past; hence their great emotion-rousing potential.

To recapitulate: the fact that art and discovery draw on unconscious sources indicates that one aspect of all creative activity is a regression to ontogenetically or philogenetically earlier levels, an escape from the restraints of the conscious mind, with the subsequent release of creative potentials—a process paralleled on lower levels by the liberation from restraint of genetic potentials or neutral equipotentiality in the regeneration of structures and functions. The scientist, traumatized by discordant facts, the artist by the pressures of sensibility, and the rat by surgical intervention, share, on different levels, the same super-flexibility enabling them to perform "adaptations of a second order," rarely found in the ordinary routines of life.

Regeneration and Creativity

I must enlarge a little on this seemingly sweeping analogy, and try to show that it is in fact based on homologous principles, traceable on all levels of the hierachy, and preserving their basic pattern throughout them.

Differentiation and specialization of the parts are necessary for the normal functioning of the whole; abnormal conditions call for radical measures which may include a retreat of the over-exerted part to a structurally less differentiated, functionally less specialized stage, if the whole is to survive. The "part" may be the newt's amputation stump, or the unsolved problem in the scientist's mind which tortures and obsesses him. We have seen that such regressions are mostly pathogenic, but under favourable conditions they may redress the situation by re-activating potentials which had been operative in the past but are inhibited in the adult—such as the regulative powers of the embryo in the womb or the undifferentiated total-pattern-responses of its nervous system. The period of incubation is a similar retreat, if not into the womb, at least into long-outgrown forms of ideation, into the pre-verbal, pre-rational games of the unconscious, the wonderland-logic of the dream. The challenge which sets the process going is in all cases a traumatic experience: physical mutilation or mental laceration—by data which do not fit, observations which contradict each other, emotions which disrupt approved styles in art: experiences which create mental conflict, dissonance, perplexity. The "creative stress" of the artist or scientist corresponds to the "general alarm reaction" of the traumatized animal; the anabolic-catabolic sequence of de-differentiation and reintegration corresponds to the destructive-constructive sequence in the creative act. The "physiological isolation" of the over-excited part which tends to dominate, corresponds to the single-minded and obsessive preoccupation with the *idée fixe*—Kretschmer's "over-valued idea," Kepler's pursuit of a chimera—which monopolizes the whole mind; it will lead either to its reorganization by giving birth to a new system, of to the cancerous proliferation of a degenerate tissue of ideas.

Over-excitation of an organ or part is one of the four causes of "physiological isolation." The other three were: growth of the whole beyond a critical limit; senescence; and (partial) blockage of communication. Each situation has its parallels on the mental plane—of the individual, or the history of thought. The unmanageable size of the total body of human knowledge—or even a single province thereof—created that dissociated phenomenon, the specialist mind; senescent cultures produce degenerate art-forms; blocked communications between Ptolemaic astronomy and the main body of the physical sciences led to the untramelled proliferation of epicycles in a closed system, divorced from reality.

"It is wonderful to see how analogies can blossom when they are given a little affection," wrote the authors of a book I have repeatedly quoted.[2] Particularly, one might add, if they have

2. G. A. Miller, E. Galanter and K. H. Pribram, *Plants and the Structure of Behavior* (New York: Holt, 1960) , p. 199.

solid roots in the earth. So let me carry analogy one step further. I have described various aspects of the Eureka process [the psychological aspect of discovery]; each of these re-structurings of thought has its obvious correlate in regenerative processes on lower levels. The "displacement of emphasis" to a previously irrelevant part or aspect of experience corresponds to the sudden dominance-of a hitherto subordinate part of an organism—such as the crab's second leg which becomes a pacemaker. The "reversal of logic" (or of the figure-background relation) has its parallel in the reversal of physiological gradients during regeneration. When psychological textbooks describe Duncker's experiments as "detaching" part of a visual percept from the context in which it is "embedded," and "attaching" it to the new context of the problem to be solved, this description itself is based on analogies from physiological processes. During incubation, the intuitive groping of ideas towards the "good combination," and their guidance by "gradients in the unconscious," reminds one of the biochemical gradients in morphogenesis, or the "contact-guidance" of out-growing nerve-processes towards their end-organ. Lastly a "nascent," unverbalized analogy may be compared to an unarticulated organ-primordium.

But these genetic skills operate only in the embryonic stage of development; in the adult they are superseded by the integrative action of the nervous system—unless the embryonic potentials are re-activated by regenerative needs. Similarly, the adult's mental coordination relies on conscious, verbalized, "logical" codes; not on the quasi "embryonic" (infantile, pre-causal) potentials of the unconscious; again unless these are revived under the creative stress. Physical regenerations strike us as "spectacular pieces of magic" because they derive from pre-natal skills; and creative inspirations are equally mysterious because they derive from levels which predate the conscious mind. As Polànyi wrote (in a different context): "The highest forms of originality are far more closely akin to the lowest biotic performances than the external circumstances would indicate."[3]

3. M. Polànyi, *Personal Knowledge* (London: Routledge & K. Paul, 1958), p. 400.

Regeneration and Evolution

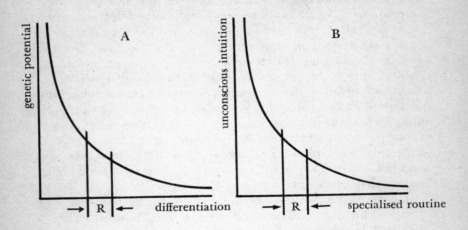

These rather fancy diagrams are solely meant to indicate in a crude way the complementary factors in the *reculer pour mieux sauter* phenomenon. In A, increase in tissue-differentiation entails a reciprocal decrease of genetic multipotentiality. In B, an analogous reciprocity prevails between unconscious intuitions and automatized routines—or, if you like, between fluid imagery and "misplaced concreteness." *R* indicates the "regenerative span." (The curve in A should of course have breaks and a series of discrete steps.)

It could be objected that structural regenerations merely restore the *status quo ante* whereas mental reorganization leads to an advance. But in the first place this is not always the case. Psychotherapy aims at correcting "faulty integrations" caused by traumatic experiences—at restoring normality. In the second place the biological evolution of the species with which we are concerned has to all intents and purposes come to a standstill, whereas mental evolution continues, and its vehicle is precisely the creative individual. The Eureka process is a mental mutation, perpetuated by social inheritance. Its biological equivalent are the genetic mutations which carried the existing species up the evolutionary ladder. Now a mutation—whatever its unknown cause—is no doubt a re-moulding of previous structures, based on a de-differentiation and reintegration of the otherwise rigid genetic code. The transformations of fins into legs, legs into arms, arms into wings, gills into lungs, scales into feathers, etc., while preserving certain basic structural patterns (see, for instance, d'Arcy Thompson's *On Growth and Form*), were eminently "witty" answers to the challenges of environment. It seems obvious that the dramatic release, at periods of adaptive radiations, of unexplored morphogenic potentials by a re-shuffling of molecules in the genetic code, resulting in the de-differentiation and reintegration of structures like limbs into wings, is of the very essence of the evolutionary process. After all, "ontogenesis and regenesis are components of a common mechanism,"[4] which must have a phylogenetic origin.

I have mentioned the perennial myth of the prophet's and hero's temporary isolation and retreat from human society— followed by his triumphant return endowed with new powers. Buddha and Mohammed go out into the desert; Joseph is thrown into the well; Jesus is resurrected from the tomb. Jung's "death and rebirth" motif, Toynbee's "withdrawal and return" reflect the same archetypal motif. It seems that *reculer pour mieux sauter* is a principle of universal validity in the evolution of species, cultures, and individuals, guiding their progression by feedback from the past.

4. A. E. Needham, in *Nature* 30 (1961), p. 12.

Abraham Maslow

The Creative Attitude

The late Abraham Maslow's lifework was involved with the search for a new understanding of human health to offset psychology's preoccupation with human sickness. One of the concepts he found useful in this effort was self-actualization, meaning the full development and expression of one's personal nature. Here Maslow explores the connection between self-actualization and creativity and describes a "creative attitude" that is not so much a source of artistic productivity as a way of life.

I

My feeling is that the concept of creativeness and the concept of the healthy, self-actualizing, fully human person seem to be coming closer together, and may perhaps turn out to be the same thing.

Another conclusion I seem to be impelled toward, even though I am not quite sure of my facts, is that creative art education, or better said, Education-Through-Art, may be especially important not so much for turning out artists or art producers as for turning out better people. If we have clearly in mind the educational goals for human beings that I will be hinting at, if we hope for our children that they will become full human beings, and that they will move toward actualizing the potentialities that they have, then, as nearly as I can make out, the

SOURCE: Reprinted with permission of *The Structurist* and the estate of Abraham H. Maslow from *The Structurist* No. 3, 1963, University of Saskatchewan, Saskatoon, Canada.

only kind of education in existence today that has any faint inkling of such goals is art education. So I am thinking of education through art not because it turns out pictures but because I think it may be possible that, clearly understood, it may become the paradigm for all other education. That is, instead of being regarded as the frill, the expendable kind of thing which it now is, if we take it seriously enough and work at it hard enough and if it turns out to be what some of us suspect it can be, then we may one day teach arithmetic and reading and writing on this paradigm. So far as I am concerned, I am talking about all education. This is why I am interested in education through art—simply because it seems to be good education in potential.

Another reason for my interest in art education, creativeness, psychological health, etc., is that I have a very strong feeling of a change of pace in history. It seems to me that we are at a point in history unike anything that has ever been before. Life moves far more rapidly now than it ever did before. Think, for instance, of the huge acceleration in the rate of growth of facts, of knowledge, of techniques, of inventions, of advances in technology. It seems very obvious to me that this requires a change in our attitude toward the human being, and toward his relationships to the world. To put it bluntly, we need a different kind of human being. I feel I must take far more seriously today than I did twenty years ago the Heraclitus, the Whitehead, the Bergson, kind of emphasis on the world as a flux, a movement, a process, not a static thing. If this is so, and it is obviously much more so than it was in 1900 or even in 1930—if this is so, then we need a different kind of human being to be able to live in a world which changes perpetually, which doesn't stand still. I may go so far as to say for the educational enterprise: What's the use of teaching facts? Facts become obsolete so darned fast! What's the use of teaching techniques? The techniques become obsolete so fast! Even the engineering schools are torn by this realization. M.I.T., for instance, no longer teaches engineering *only* as the acquisition of a series of skills, because practically all the skills that the professors of engineering learned when they were in school have now become obsolete. It's no use today learning to make buggy whips. What some professors have done at M.I.T., I understand, is to give up the teaching of the tried and true methods of the past, in favor of trying to create a new kind of human being who is comfortable with change, who enjoys change, who is able to improvise, who is able to face with confidence, strength, and courage a situation of which he has absolutely no forewarning.

Even today *everything* seems to be changing; international law is changing, politics are changing, the whole international scene is changing. People talk with each other in the United Nations from across different centuries. One man speaks in terms of the international law of the nineteenth century. Another one answers him in terms of something else entirely, from a different platform in a different world. Things have changed that fast.

To come back to my title, what I'm talking about is the job of trying to make ourselves over into people who don't need to staticize the world, who don't need to freeze it and to make it stable, who don't need to do what their daddies did, who are able confidently to face tomorrow not knowing what's going to come, not knowing what will happen, with confidence enough in ourselves that we will be able to improvise in that situation which has never existed before. This means a new type of human being. Heraclitian, you might call him. The society which can turn out such people will survive; the societies that *cannot* turn out such people will die.

You'll notice that I stress a great deal improvising and inspiration, rather than approaching creativeness from the vantage point of the finished work of art, of the great creative work. As a matter of fact, I won't even approach it today from the point of view of completed products at all. Why is this? Because we're pretty clearly aware now, from our psychological analysis of the process of creativeness and of creative individuals, that we must make the distinction between primary creativeness and a secondary creativeness. The primary creativeness, or the inspirational phase of creativeness, must be separated from the working out and the development of the inspiration. This is because the latter phase stresses not only creativeness, but also relies very much on just plain hard work, on the discipline of the artist who may spend half a lifetime learning his tools, his skills, and his materials, until he becomes finally ready for a full expression of what he sees. I am very certain that many, many people have waked up in the middle of the night with a flash of inspiration about some novel they would like to write, or a play or a poem or whatever, and that most of these inspirations never came to anything. Inspirations are a dime a dozen. The difference between the inspiration and the final product, for example, Tolstoy's *War and Peace*, is an awful lot of hard work, an awful lot of discipline, an awful lot of training, an awful lot of finger exercises and practices and rehearsals and throwing away first drafts and so on. Now the virtues which go with the secondary kind of creativeness, the creativeness which results in the actual products, in the great paintings, the great novels, in the bridges, the new inventions, and so on, rest as heavily upon other virtues—stubbornness and patience and hard work and so on—as they do upon the creativeness of the personality. Therefore, in order to keep the field of operation clean, you might say, it seems necessary to me to focus upon improvising on this first flash and, for the moment, not to worry about what becomes of it, recognizing that many of them do get lost. Partly for this reason, among the best subjects to study for this inspirational phase of creativeness are young children whose inventiveness and creativeness very frequently cannot be defined in terms of product. When a little boy discovers the decimal system for himself this can be a high moment of inspiration, and a high creative moment, and should not be waved aside because of some *a priori* definition which says creativeness ought to be socially useful or it ought to be novel, or nobody should have thought of it before, etc.

For this same reason I have decided for myself not to take scientific creativeness as a paradigm, but rather to use other examples. Much of the research that's going on now deals with the creative scientists, with people who have proven themselves to be creative, Nobel prize winners, great inventors, and so on. The trouble is, if you know a lot of scientists, that you soon learn that something is wrong with this criterion because scientists as a group are not nearly as creative generally as you would expect. This includes people who have discovered, who have created actually, who have published things which were advances in human knowledge. Actually, this is not too difficult to understand. This finding tells us something about the nature of science rather than about the nature of creativeness. If I wanted to be mischievous about it, I could go so far as to define science as a technique whereby noncreative people can create. This is by no means making fun of scientists. It's a wonderful thing it seems to me, for limited human beings, that they can be pressed into the service of great things even though they themselves are not great people. Science is a technique, social and institutionalized, whereby even unintelligent people can be useful in the advance of knowledge. That is as extreme and dramatic as I can make it. Since any particular scientist rests so much in the arms of history, stands on so many shoulders of so many predecessors, he is so much a part of a huge basketball team, of a big collection of people, that his own shortcomings may not appear. He becomes worthy of reverence, worthy of great respect through his participation in a great and respectworthy enterprise. Therefore, when he discovers something, I have learned to understand this as a product of a social institution, of a collaboration. If he didn't discover it, somebody else would have pretty soon. Therefore, it seems to me that selecting our scientists, even though they have created, is not the best way to study the theory of creativeness.

I believe also that we cannot study creativeness in an ultimate sense until we realize that practically all the definitions that we have been using of creativeness, and most of the examples of creativeness that we use, are essentially male or masculine products. We've left out of consideration almost entirely the creativeness of women by the simple semantic technique of defining only male products as creative and overlooking entirely the creativeness of women. I have learned recently (through my studies of peak experiences) to look to women and to feminine creativeness as a good field of operation for research, because it gets less involved in products, less involved in achievement, more involved with the process itself, with the going-on process rather than with the climax in obvious triumph and success.

This is the background of the particular problem I am talking about.

II

The puzzle that I'm now trying to unravel is suggested by the observation that the creative person, in the inspirational phase of the creative furor, loses his past and his future and lives only in the moment. He is all there, totally immersed, fascinated and absorbed in the present, in the current situation, in the here-now, with the matter-in-hand. Or to use a perfect phrase from *The Spinster* by Sylvia Ashton-Warner, the teacher absorbed with a new method of teaching reading to her children says, "I am utterly lost in the present."

This ability to become "lost in the present" seems to be a *sine qua non* for creativeness of any kind. But also certain *prerequisites* of creativeness—in whatever realm—somehow have something to do with this ability to become timeless, selfless, outside of space, of society, of history.

It has begun to appear strongly that this phenomenon is a diluted, more secular, more frequent version of the mystical experience that has been described so often as to have become what Huxley called *The Perennial Philosophy*. In various cultures and in various eras, it takes on somewhat different coloration—and yet its essence is always recognizable—it is the same.

It is always described as a loss of self or of ego, or sometimes as a transcendence of self. There is a fusion with the reality being observed (with the matter-in-hand, I shall say more neutrally), a oneness where there was a twoness, an integration of some sort of the self with the non-self. There is universally reported a seeing of formerly hidden truth, a revelation in the strict sense, a stripping away of veils, and finally, almost always, the whole experience is experienced as bliss, ecstasy, rapture, exaltation.

Little wonder that this shaking experience has so often been considered to be superhuman, supernatural, so much greater and grander than anything conceivable as human that it could only be attributed to trans-human sources. And such "revelations" often serve as basis, sometimes the *sole* basis, for the various "revealed" religions.

And yet even this most remarkable of all experiences has now been brought into the realm of human experience and cognition. My researches on what I call peak experiences,[1] and Marghanita

---

1. Abraham H. Maslow, "Lessons from the Peak Experiences," *Journal of Humanistic Psychology* 2 (1962), pp. 9–18; *idem, Toward a Psychology of Being* (Princeton, N.J.: D. Van Nostrand Company, 1962; rev. ed., 1968).

Laski's on what she calls ecstasies,[2] done quite independently of each other, show that these experiences are quite naturalistic, quite easily investigated, and, what is to the point right now, that they have much to teach us about creativeness as well as other aspects of the full functioning of human beings when they are most fully realizing themselves, most mature and evolved, most healthy, when, in a word, they are most fully human.

One main characteristic of the peak experience is just this total fascination with the matter-in-hand, this getting lost in the present, this detachment from time and place. And it seems to me now that much of what we have learned from the study of these peak experiences can be transferred quite directly to the enriched understanding of the here-now experience, of the creative attitude.

It is not necessary for us to confine ourselves to these uncommon and rather extreme experiences, even though it now seems clear that practically all people can report moments of rapture if they dig around long enough in their memories, and if the interview situation is just right. We can also refer to the simplest version of the peak experience, namely, fascination, concentration, or absorption in *anything* which is interesting enough to hold this attention completely. And I mean not only great symphonies or tragedies; the job can be done by a gripping movie or detective story, or simply becoming absorbed with one's work. There are certain advantages in starting from such universal and familiar experiences which we all have, so that we can get a direct feeling or intuition or empathy, that is, a direct experimental knowledge of a modest, moderate version of the fancier "high" experiences. For one thing we can avoid the flossy, high-flying, extremely metaphorical vocabulary that is so common in this realm.

Well then, what are some of the things that happen in these moments?

Giving Up the Past. The best way to view a present problem is to give it all you've got, to study *it* and its nature, to perceive *within* it the intrinsic interrelationships, to discover (rather than to invent) the answer to the problem within the problem itself.

2. Marghanita Laski, *Ecstasy* (London: Cresset Press, 1961).

This is also the best way to look at a painting or to listen to a patient in therapy.

The other way is merely a matter of shuffling over past experiences, past habits, past knowledge to find out in what respects this current situation is similar to some situation in the past, i.e., to classify it, and then to use *now* the solution that once worked for the similar problem in the past. This can be likened to the work of a filing clerk. I have called it "rubricizing."[3] And it works well enough to the extent that the present *is* like the past.

But obviously it *doesn't* work insofar as the matter-in-hand is different from the past. The file-clerk approach fails then. This person confronting an unknown painting hurriedly runs back through his knowledge of art history to remember how he is to react. Meanwhile of course he is hardly looking at the painting. All he needs is the name or the style or the content to enable him to do his quick calculations. He then enjoys it if he is supposed to, and doesn't if he is *not* supposed to.

In such a person, the past is an inert, undigested foreign body which the person carries about. It is not yet the person himself.

More accurately said: The past is active and alive only insofar as it has re-created the person, and has been digested into the present person. It is not or should not be something *other* than the person, something alien to it. It has now become Person (and has lost its own identity as something different and other), just as past steaks that I have eaten are now me, *not* steaks. The digested past (assimilated by intussusception) is different from the undigested past. It is Lewin's "ahistorical past."

Giving Up the Future. Often we use the present not for its own sake but in order to prepare for the future. Think how often in a conversation we put on a listening face as the other person talks, secretly however preparing what we are going to say, rehearsing, planning a counterattack perhaps. Think how different your attitude would be right now if you knew you were to comment on my remarks in five minutes. Think how hard it would be then to be a good, total listener.

If we are totally listening or totally looking, we have thereby

3. Abraham H. Maslow, *Motivation and Personality* (New York: Harper & Brothers, 1954; rev. ed., 1970).

given up this kind of "preparing for the future." We don't treat the present as merely a means to some future end (thereby devaluating the present). And obviously, this kind of forgetting the future is a prerequisite to total involvement with the present. Just as obviously, a good way to "forget" the future is not to be apprehensive about it.

Of course, this is only one sense of the concept "future." The future which is within us, part of our present selves, is another story altogether.[4]

Innocence. This amounts to a kind of "innocence" of perceiving and behaving. Something of the sort has often been attributed to highly creative people. They are variously described as being naked in the situation, guileless, without *a priori* expectations, without "shoulds" or "oughts," without fashions, fads, dogmas, habits, or other pictures-in-the-head of what is proper, normal, "right," as being ready to receive whatever happens to be the case without surprise, shock, indignation, or denial.

Children are more able to be receptive in this undemanding way. So are wise old people. And it appears now that we *all* may be more innocent in this style when we become "here-now."

Narrowing of Consciousness. We have now become much less conscious of everything other than the matter-in-hand (less distractible). *Very* important here is our lessened awareness of other people, of their ties to us and ours to them, of obligations, duties, fears, hopes, etc. We become much more free of other people, which in turn, means that we become much more ourselves, our Real Selves (Horney), our authentic selves, our real identity.

This is so because *the* greatest cause of our alienation from our real selves is our neurotic involvements with other people, the historical hangovers from childhood, the irrational transferences, in which past and present are confused, and in which the adult acts like a child. (By the way, it's all right for the *child* to act like a child. His dependencies on other people can be very real. *But*, after all, he *is* supposed to outgrow them. To be afraid of what daddy will say or do is certainly out of place if daddy has been dead for twenty years.)

4. Maslow, *Toward a Psychology of Being*, pp. 14–15.

In a word, we become more free of the influence of other people in such moments. So, insofar as these influences have affected our behavior, they no longer do so.

This means dropping masks, dropping our efforts to influence, to impress, to please, to be lovable, to win applause. It could be said so: If we have no audience to play to, we cease to be actors. With no need to act we can devote ourselves, self-forgetfully, to the problem.

Loss of Ego: Self-Forgetfulness, Loss of Self-Consciousness. When you are totally absorbed in non-self, you tend to become less conscious of yourself, less self-aware. You are less apt to be observing yourself like a spectator or a critic. To use the language of psychodynamics, you become less dissociated than usual into a self-observing ego and an experiencing ego; i.e., you come much closer to being *all* experiencing ego. (You tend to lose the shyness and bashfulness of the adolescent, the painful awareness of being looked at, etc.) This in turn means more unifying, more oneness and integration of the person.

It also means less criticizing and editing, less evaluating, less selecting and rejecting, less judging and weighing, less splitting and analyzing of the experience.

This kind of self-forgetfulness is one of the paths to finding one's true identity, one's real self, one's authentic nature, one's deepest nature. It is almost felt as pleasant and desirable. We needn't go so far as the Buddhists and Eastern thinkers do in talking about the "accursed ego"; and yet there *is* something in what they say.

Inhibiting Force of Consciousness (of Self). In some senses consciousness (especially of self) is inhibiting in some ways and at some times. It is sometimes the locus of doubts, conflicts, fears, etc. It is sometimes harmful to full-functioning creativeness. It is sometimes an inhibitor of spontaneity and of expressiveness (*but* the observing ego is necessary for therapy) .

And yet it is also true that some kind of self-awareness, self-observation, self-criticism—i.e., the self-observing ego—*is* necessary for "secondary creativeness." To use psychotherapy as an example, the task of self-improvement is partly a consequence of criticizing the experiences that one has allowed to come into consciousness. Schizophrenic people experience many insights and yet don't make therapeutic use of them because they are too much "totally experiencing" and not enough "self-observing-and-criticizing." In creative work, likewise, the labor of disciplined construction succeeds upon the phase of "inspiration."

Fears Disappear. This means that our fears and anxieties also tend to disappear. So also our depressions, conflicts, ambivalence, our worries, our problems, even our physical pains. Even—for the moment—our psychoses and our neuroses (that is, if they are not so extreme as to prevent us from becoming deeply interested and immersed in the matter-in-hand) .

For the time being, we are courageous and confident, unafraid, unanxious, unneurotic, not sick.

Lessening of Defenses and Inhibitions. Our inhibitions also tend to disappear. So also our guardedness, our (Freudian) defenses, and controls (brakes) on our impulses as well as the defenses against danger and threat.

Strength and Courage. The creative attitude requires both courage and strength, and most studies of creative people have reported one or another version of courage: stubbornness, independence, self-sufficiency, a kind of arrogance, strength of character, ego-strength, etc.; popularity becomes a minor consideration. Fear and weakness cast out creativeness or at least make it less likely.

It seems to me that this aspect of creativeness becomes somewhat more understandable when it is seen as a part of the syndrome of here-now self-forgetfulness and other-forgetfulness. Such a state intrinsically implies less fear, less inhibition, less need for defense and self-protection, less guardedness, less need for artificiality, less fear of ridicule, of humiliation and of failure. All these characteristcs are *part of* self-forgetfulness and audience-forgetfulness. Absorption casts out fear.

Or we can say, in a more positive way, that becoming more courageous makes it easier to let oneself be attracted by mystery, by the unfamiliar, by the novel, by the ambiguous and contradictory, by the unusual and unexpected, etc., instead of becoming suspicious, fearful, guarded, or having to throw into action our anxiety-allaying mechanisms and defenses.

Acceptance: The Positive Attitude. In moments of here-now immersion and self-forgetfulness we are apt to become more "positive" and less negative in still another way, namely, in giving up criticism (editing, picking and choosing, correcting, skepticism, improving, doubting, rejecting, judging, evaluating) . This is like saying that we accept. We don't reject or disapprove or selectively pick and choose.

No blocks against the matter-in-hand means that we let it flow in upon us. We let it wreak its will upon us. We let it have its way. We let it be itself. Perhaps we can even approve of its being itself.

This makes it easier to be Taoistic in the sense of humility, noninterference, receptivity.

Trust vs. Trying, Controlling, Striving. All of the foregoing happenings imply a kind of trust in the self and a trust in the world which permits the temporary giving up of straining and striving, of volition and control, of conscious coping and effort. To permit oneself to be determined by the intrinsic nature of the matter-in-hand here-now necessarily implies relaxation, waiting, receiving. The common effort to master, to dominate, and to control are antithetical to a true coming-to-terms with or a true perceiving of the materials (or the problem, or the person, etc.) . Especially is this true with respect to the future. We *must* trust our ability to improvise when confronted with novelty in the future. Phrased in this way, we can see more clearly that trust involves self-confidence, courage, lack of fear of the world. It is also clear that this kind of trust in ourselves-facing-the-unknown-future is a condition of being able to turn totally, nakedly, and wholeheartedly to the present.

(Some clinical examples may help. Giving birth, urination, defecation, sleeping, floating in the water, sexual surrender are all instances in which straining, trying, controlling, have to be given up in favor of relaxed, trusting, confident letting things happen.)

Taoistic Receptivity. Both Taoism and receptivity mean many things, all of them important, but also subtle and difficult to convey except in figures of speech. All of the subtle and delicate Taoistic attributes of the creative attitude which follow have been described again and again by the many writers on creativeness, now in one way, now in another. However, everyone agrees that in the primary or inspirational phase of creativeness, some degree of receptivity or noninterference or "let-be" is descriptively characteristic and also theoretically and dynamically necessary. Our question now is how does this receptivity or "letting things happen" relate to the syndrome of here-now immersion and self-forgetfulness?

For one thing, using the artist's respect for his materials as a paradigm, we may speak of this respectful attention to the matter-in-hand as a kind of courtesy or deference (without intrusion of the controlling will) which is akin to "taking it seriously." This amounts to treating it as an end, something *per se*, with its own right to be, rather than as a means to some end other than itself; i.e., as a tool for some extrinsic purpose. This respectful treatment of its being implies that it is respectworthy.

This courtesy or respectfulness can apply equally to the problem, to the materials, to the situation, or to the person. It is what one writer (Follett) has called deference (yielding, surrender) to the authority of the facts, to the law of the situation. I can go over from a bare *permitting* "it" to be itself, to a loving, caring, approving, joyful *eagerness* that it be itself, as with one's child or sweetheart or tree or poem or pet animal.

Some such attitude is *a priori* necessary for perceiving or understanding the full concrete richness of the matter-in-hand, in *its* own nature and in *its* own style, without our help, without our imposing ourselves upon it, in about the same way that we must hush and be still if we wish to hear the whisper from the other. . . .

Integration of the B-Cognizer (vs. Dissociation). Creating tends to be the act of a whole man (ordinarily); he is then *most* integrated, unified, all of a piece, one-pointed, totally organized in the service of the fascinating matter-in-hand. Creativeness is therefor systemic; i.e., a whole—or Gestalt—quality of the whole person; it is not added-to the organism like a coat of paint, or like an invasion of bacteria. It is the opposite of dissociation. Here-now-allness is less dissociated (split) and more one.

Permission to Dip into Primary Process. Part of the process of integration of the person is the recovery of aspects of the unconscious and preconscious, particularly of the primary process (or poetic, metaphoric, mystic, primitive, archaic, childlike). Our conscious intellect is too exclusively analytic, rational, numerical, atomistic, conceptual, and so it misses a great deal of reality, especially within ourselves.

Aesthetic Perceiving Rather Than Abstracting. Abstracting is more active and interfering (less Taoistic); more selecting-rejecting than the aesthetic (Northrop) attitude of savoring, enjoying, appreciating, caring, in a noninterfering, nonintruding, noncontrolling way.

The end product of abstracting is the mathematical equation, the chemical formula, the map, the diagram, the blueprint, the cartoon, the concept, the abstracting sketch, the model, the theoretical system, all of which move further and further from raw reality ("the map is *not* the territory"). The end product of aesthetic perceiving, of nonabstracting, is the total inventory of the percept, in which everything in it is apt to be equally savored, and in which evaluations of more important and less important tend to be given up. Here greater richness of the percept is sought for rather than greater simplifying and skeletonizing.

For many confused scientists and philosophers, the equation, the concept, or the blueprint have become more real than the phenomenological reality itself. Fortunately now that we can understand the interplay and mutual enrichment of the concrete and the abstract, it is no longer necessary to devalue one or the other. For the moment, we intellectuals in the West who have heavily and exclusively overvalued abstractness in our picture of reality, even to the point of synonymizing them, had better redress the balance by stressing concrete, aesthetic, phenomenological, nonabstracting perceiving of *all* the aspects and details of phenomena, of the full richness of reality, including the useless portions of it.

Fullest Spontaneity. If we are fully concentrated on the matter-in-hand, fascinated with it for its own sake, having no other goals or purposes in mind, then it is easier to be fully spontaneous, fully functioning, letting our capacities flow forth easily from within, of themselves, without effort, without conscious volition or control, in an instinct-like, automatic, thoughtless way; i.e., the fullest, least obstructed, most organized action.

The one main determinant of their organization and adaptation to the matter-in-hand is then most apt to be the intrinsic nature of the matter-in-hand. Our capacities then adapt to the situation most perfectly, quickly, effortlessly, and change flexibly as the situation changes; e.g., a painter continuously adapts himself to the demands of his developing painting; as a wrestler adapts himself to his opponent; as a pair of fine dancers mutually adapt to each other; as water flows into cracks and contours.

Fullest Expressiveness (of Uniqueness). Full spontaneity is a guarantee of honest expression of the nature and the style of the freely functioning organism, and of its uniqueness. Both words, spontaneity and expressiveness, imply honesty, naturalness, truthfulness, lack of guile, nonimitativeness, etc., because they also imply a noninstrumental nature of the behavior, a lack of willful "trying," a lack of effortful striving or straining, a lack of interference with the flow of the impulses and the free "radiating" expression of the deep person.

The only determinants now are the intrinsic nature of the matter-in-hand, the intrinsic nature of the person and the intrinsic necessities of their fluctuating adaptation to each other to form a fusion, a unit; e.g., a fine basketball team, or a string quartet. Nothing outside this fusion situation is relevant. The situation is not a means to any extrinsic end; it is an end in itself.

Fusion of the Person with the World. We wind up with the fusion between the person and his world which has so often been reported as an observable fact in creativeness, and which we may now reasonably consider to be a *sine qua non*. I think that this spider web of interrelationships that I have been teasing apart and discussing can help us to understand this fusion better as a natural event, rather than as something mysterious, arcane, esoteric. I think it can even be researched if we understand it to be an isomorphism, a molding of each to each other, a better and better fitting together or complementarity, a melting into one.

It has helped me to understand what Hokusai meant when he said, "If you want to draw a bird, you must become a bird."

The Arts in Therapy

Eric Bentley

·———·

Theatre and Therapy

*I have worked with psychodrama for nearly a decade, and during that
time I have read a good deal of literature on the subject. I know of
no better introduction to it than this essay by a perceptive drama
critic who looked at psychodrama with an outsider's eyes and asked
some questions about the connections (and the distinctions) between
drama as therapy and drama as entertainment.*

For better or for worse, the principal event of the 1968–1969
theatre season was the visit to New York of the Living Theatre.
Of their offering, they made a kind of take-it-or-leave-it prop-
osition. I was one of those who "left it," but not in the sense that
I left off thinking about it. What I propose to pursue here is the
question: What has all the talk of the Living Theatre and kin-
dred theatres really been about?

There is no one correct answer, but a central topic has certainly
been "audience involvement." The Living Theatre was trying to
change the character of the theatrical event. They wanted to move
the audience onto the stage. They wanted to exercise a therapeutic influence. On the audience, of course; but also, as they
proclaimed, on themselves: the audience was to help cure *them*.
I asked myself when had I heard something of the sort before.
The whole conception seemed to be one of group therapy, rather
than theatre as previously conceived, but had not one celebrated
group therapist already effected a merger of these two, and, in

SOURCE: From *Theatre of War* by Eric Bentley. Copyright © 1970 by
Eric Bentley. Reprinted by permission of The Viking Press, Inc.

his system, was the actor not indeed the patient, and did not the audience assist in treating him?

The therapist was Jacob Levy Moreno; his name was in the Manhattan phone book, and I had no difficulty getting myself invited to attend the group-therapy sessions of the Moreno Institute on West Seventy-eighth Street. Meanwhile I was seeing various shows around town that claimed to be doing something special with audience participation, and/or trying to give theatre a push toward therapy. I saw *The Concept, The Serpent, Dionysus in 69.* . . . Even the current nudism proved relevant. Insofar as it was more than a pursuit of a quick buck, it was an affirmation of the body, the health of the body, and was related to "nude therapy," sensitivity training, encounter groups, etc. I visited some of these groups and also saw *Hair, The Sound of a Different Drum, We'd Rather Switch, Geese, Che, Oh! Calcutta!,* and so on. Of the theatres, I think the Play-house of the Ridiculous and the Ridiculous Theatrical Company were probably the most cathartic, being founded on the deepest rejection of The American Way, and inspired with the cockiest faith that they can get along without imitating that form of life. But gradually I found myself seeing shows less and Moreno's "psychodramas" more. If one wanted therapy in the theatre, why not go the whole hog? At the Moreno Institute, therapy was the acknowledged and sole aim in view, yet the sessions there were emotionally affecting and intellectually interesting to a much greater degree than the New York theatres. What more did I want?

For the moment, nothing. And I concluded that, rather than attempt any sort of survey of the new trend in theatre, I would simply try to explain what is at stake. Should drama be psychodrama? Is psychodramatic therapy the same as dramatic art? Are certain mergers called for? Or are certain separations—certain firm distinctions—in order? If we could attain to a degree of clarity on these matters, "current trends on and off Broadway" would be child's play.

Since it was psychodrama that prompted this approach and underpins the reasoning that follows, it will be as well to state in advance just what a psychodramatic session is. Perhaps a hundred people are placed on three sides of a platform. The platform itself has steps on all sides, is in this sense an "open stage." A patient, here called a protagonist, presents himself for a psycho-dramatic performance. A director-psychiatrist talks with him briefly, to find out what he sees as his problem, and what scenes from his life might be enacted. A scene being chosen, the roles of others taking part in it are played either by trained assistants or by anyone else present who might volunteer. What and how they are to play is briefly explained to them by the protagonist and director. If they then seem too far wide of the mark, the protagonist may reject them. But in each session, successful scenes do develop, "success" here being measured by the degree of spontaneity attained: if the protagonist does not "warm up" to his role, he cannot play it in its vital fullness.

Generalizations about the course of psychodramatic sessions are hazardous, since one session differs widely from another, but a typical line of development would be from relatively trivial scenes with friends in the recent past to serious and crucial scenes with parents in the more distant past. It will often happen that a protagonist will have an illumination, or at least a surprise, in one of these later scenes. He may suddenly realize that where he had seen only love there was also hate, or vice versa, in one of his main relationships. And here the stress should be on the word "realize," for it is likely to be a powerful emotional expe-rience: a given insight is borne in upon a person in the midst of a very lively distress. The distress has opened the channels of communication. It may also have reached a kind of climax. The patient may, for the time being, feel cleaned out. The director now ends the play-acting and asks the audience to share common experience with the protagonist. The point is not to elicit inter-pretations but to discover what chords were touched in the on-lookers, what degree of therapy was in it all for them.

I

Dramatic art and psychodramatic therapy have a common source in the fact that life itself is dramatic. In other words, life is not a shapeless stuff which is given form only by a dramatist or clinician. Human life, like the rest of nature, has been shaped, indeed so markedly that this shaping has always been the leading argument for the existence of God. As the beauty of leaves or seashells is attributed to God the Creator, so the shape of events, large or small, is attributed to God the Dramatist: life, as Dante classically stated it, is a divine comedy. The idea that "all the world's a stage/And all the men and women merely players" is not a clever improvisation casually tossed off by Shakespeare's cynic Jaques, it was written on the wall of Shakespeare's theatre, the Globe, in a language older than English: *Totus mundus facit histrionem.* To speak of life, as many modern psychiatrists do, as role-playing is only to make a new phrase, not to advance a new idea.

I shall return later to role-playing and would only at this point call attention to the positive side of the pattern. The negative side is all too familiar: it is that people are often hypocritical—use a role to pretend to be better than they are and deceive other people. It is curious how the phrase "play-acting" has come to be a slur: it implies insincereity. Yet the commonplaces I have cited imply that one has no alternative to play-acting. The choice is only between one role and another. And this is precisely the positive side of the idea: that we do have a choice, that life does offer us alternatives, that one's will is free within whatever limits, and the end is not yet determined. Life is not merely going through the motions, it is an adventure: which is often all that people mean by calling it dramatic.

What else might they mean? In the vernacular, these days, "dramatic" means little more than thrilling, and if it also means "spectacular" the sense of an actual theatrical spectacle is probably not intended. Dramatist and psychodramatist give the term "dramatic" a much more elaborate interpretation. Just as they see more roles to role-playing than Jaques's seven, they break down the "stage" which "all the world" is said to be into various departments. Given that there are roles to play, how are they played? A full answer to this question would be by way of a description of myriad different roles and relationships. A short answer, aiming at providing a basic scheme, might run somewhat as follows.

A role is properly and fully played by being brought into living contact with another role played by another actor. The "full" playing of the role implies that living contact is made, that if "I" am playing one role, "I" feel that the other role is a "Thou" and not an "It." (I am using terminology that most people will associate with Martin Buber, though J. L. Moreno has long thought along these lines too.) Buber's point has been that the modern person reacts to others as an It, and so forestalls communication. "I," too, become an It, if the other is an It. Neurosis walls us off from each other. That's modern life.

Now drama does not depict a utopia in which neurosis is absent, but, with an exception to be noted in a minute, it is utopian to the extent that it normally, not exceptionally, shows human beings in living contact with each other, shows couples who are "I" and "Thou" to each other. It may be living hatred that communicates, as in Strindberg's *Father,* or love, as in *Romeo and Juliet,* but that there *is* direct and lively communication is not only obvious, it is what interests us, it is what we want from theatre. Could it be said, then, that life is not dramatic in this respect, only theatre is? Perhaps. But the point is that this is a norm, not just for our theatregoing, but for our living. The "I" and "Thou" relationship is present enough in actual life for us to want to see more of it, and when we do see it in the theatre, our attitude need not be, "but that's because theatre is not life" but rather "this is what is trying to happen in life if only we would let it." For art need not be regarded as a more abundant life, but unreal. It can be regarded as an attempt by the life force (or what have you) to make our real life more abundant.

If life does afford real I/Thou relationships, and also, which is crucial, holds out the hope of ever more successful I/Thou relationships, drama can, for its part, portray the failure to achieve such relationships. But how could this possibly prove dramatic? Wouldn't the absence of live contact kill the stage action stone dead? It would—if nothing else is added. Drama characterized by a mere absence of emotion is dead. Suppose, however, the absence of emotion, of flow, is the very point? That, you say, is ridiculous. Then, I reply, the way to give it life is to give it ridiculous life. The dramatic form which regularly presents people who are out of contact with each other is the art of comedy, whose mode is ridicule. The role-playing in *The Importance of Being Earnest* is all a game of pretending to have living I/Thou relationships—friend to friend, parent to child, man to woman—when such relationships are not in the cards. Again, when we say comedy presents types, not individuals, we might just as well say it presents individuals who cannot make contact with other individuals because of a crust of nonindividual class characteristics. This is not a *man*, Molière or Shaw is forcing us to say, it is a *doctor*.

The question whether tragedy or comedy is closer to life becomes rather a snarled one. Tragedy presents us in our emotional fullness; it has, therefore, more of life in it. Comedy presents our customary failure to live that way and, in presenting less of life, gives a more characteristic version of it. As for I/Thou relationships, if they are per se dramatic, then we may say that life aspires to the condition of drama.

Does the I/Thou relationship, granted that it includes role-playing, amount to drama? If we would be inclined to say yes, that is becauce we have taken ourselves for granted. *We* are watching the "I" and the "Thou." We are their audience, and from their viewpoint a "They." Theatre is this completed circuit: an "I" and a "Thou" on stage and a "They" out front. Which is a very radical, if schematic, version of the rudiments of living: *I* relate to *you,* while *they* watch. I, Romeo, relate to you, Juliet, while the other Montagues and Capulets watch. This example, if extreme, serves to remind us how much those watchful eyes modify the I/Thou experience. We live out our lives in full view of other people. We do not live in a world of our own. We live in "their" world. How much tragedy, both of life and literature, lurks in that formula!

II

This, at any rate, is the image of life which psychodrama has appropriated: an "I," talking on stage to a "Thou," in front of a "They." By that token, psychodrama may be said to resemble life or even to be a slice (many slices) of it. Visitors are surprised how close it comes to the real thing. And its watchword is spontaneity. Nonetheless, psychodrama has to depart from life in a number of ways, notably:

1. The "I" is not presented in a sheer, naked, literal state but

buttressed, clothed, supplemented by another person. When the protagonist, at a psychodramatic session, is found to be reluctant, silent, overdefensive, another person is asked to play his double and to come forward with exactly those responses which the protagonist is holding back. Thus, to take a crude instance, in the matter of ambivalence, if the protagonist keeps saying, I *love* my mother," and clamming up, the double will say, "I hate her guts." This is as different from life as can be, since help is being given precisely where it was, perhaps disastrously, lacking. (The double can of course guess wrong, but this fact will probably emerge from what the protagonist then says and does. In any case, there is nothing definitive in a possibly false suggestion. The situation remains open.)

2. The "Thou" is rendered in more or less the form not of life but of drama, namely: impersonation. Any partner the protagonist's story requires is enacted either by a trained assistant or by a member of the audience at the session in question. Since this is a "stranger" to the protagonist, the difference, for him, from the real thing is very great indeed. Often it is necessary for the protagonist to reject outright what the player of such a role says. Sometimes he has to have him replaced. "My father just wouldn't react that way."

But—and this is what matters—some degree of I/Thou relationship is generally worked out before a session is over. Indeed what needs calling attention to is not the difficulty of reaching a degree of direct communication under the conditions of a psychodramatic session but the fact that life is outdone by psychodrama in this respect, somewhat as it is by dramatic art, though not by as much. It must be galling, for example, for a parent to learn how his child enters into rapport with a substitute parent far more readily than with the real one, but a moment's thought explains this: the "objection" is precisely to the real parent, and the "false" one is the real one minus the objection. Hence psychodrama is not "naturalistic," is not a duplication of actuality but, in the most relevant way, an improvement on it in exactly the same way as nonnaturalistic art is, for nonnaturalistic art is not merely reproduced, but interpreted normatively, which means: to a certain extent transformed. Psychodrama and drama have in common a thrust toward human *liberation*.

To take up a single example. When a person fails to communicate with his nearest and dearest, he is apt to reach the extreme conclusion: "If I cannot reach them, I can reach no one." Actually, it is only they whom he cannot reach. the rest of the human race is more accessible. And psychodrama is not an argument to this effect but the living proof written in letters of emotion upon a person's whole nervous system: the kind of proof even philosophers don't easily reject when it's their own nervous system that is responding.

The form taken by scenes created in psychodramatic sessions stands, correspondingly, at a remove from actuality. The patient-protagonist is not encouraged to rack his brains for accuracy in reporting, as when someone tries to be very honest and self-disciplined in telling the police what occurred on a given occasion. What he does, after reminding himself as vividly as possible of the actual moment and location, is to let go and *throw* himself into the situation with a lack of reservation that at the time he hadn't actually achieved. Thus what is "brought back" from that actual happening is, in one sense, more than was there in the first place—more than was *known* to be there, more than actually emerged. Which is, of course, the reason for going to all the trouble. Mere rehash is a waste of energy for the rehasher, as well as being a great bore for those who have to listen. But I shall leave further comment on the psychology of recapitulation till later. The point here is that the "Thou" who is less, in that he may be a mere stranger, is also more, in that he is really a "Thou" where the nonstrangers were not.

3. A third way in which psychodrama deviates from life is in making use of a director. There are few who feel, these days, that the drama of their lives is directed by God. That was hard to believe with any constancy at any time; today, if there is a God at all, He is an absentee landlord, a director on perpetual sick leave abandoning the actors to their own resources. Jacob Moreno, though, always wanted to play God, and the modern age obviously placed no special obstacles in his path. He modestly called himself—or any of his standbys—directors; but they preside over the psychodramatic sessions in fairly godlike fashion.

In psychodramatic sessions, the director intervenes in several ways. In the beginning, he elicits the information on the basis of which a first scene is set up. He then *interrupts* whenever it seems to him the drama is (*a*) repeating itself, (*b*) wandering off, or (*c*) petering out. Since anyone could easily be wrong on any of these three matters, it is clear that considerable shrewdness is called for, not to mention knowledge. Interruption is, in any event, a very dynamic factor in itself, as some playwrights (e.g., Brecht) have known. It gives a jolt, which can be salutary or disastrous according to the moment when it occurs.

Interruption is the director's chief negative act. But he does something positive, too, and usually right after the interruption: he *suggests* an alternative path. Having stopped the patient-protagonist from pursuing one course, he propels him into another. Again, the possibility of error is considerable, but again much can be expected from knowledge and know-how. And again, errors need not be final. On the contrary, given the patient's set of mind, they will probably be exposed rather soon. A dead end is a dead end, and is seen to be so by patient and/or audience.

In one sense, then, the director is *not* called on to be God and always right, but only to be resourceful and always quick. The right moment to reach a stop or institute a change passes fast. The director must have instantaneous reactions that indicate immediate conclusions such as: "This is when a double is needed," "We must go straight to the scene just suggested in the dialogue," "Let's reverse roles here."

Reversal of roles, incidentally, is one of the chief devices of psychodrama, and perhaps one of the most efficacious. At a word from the director, the protagonist plays the "other fellow" in the scene. Thus "I" is forced to see and feel out the situation from the viewpoint of "Thou." Which is not only morally edifying but generally illuminating and specifically therapeutic. Our whole failure as human beings can be found in the failure to take in the reality of the other person. But merely knowing this doesn't help. Psychodrama can help by the *work* involved in "I"'s playing seriously at being "Thou."

In a sense, too, the director is not outsde the psychodrama, but inside it. His is a voice that the patient sorely lacked the *first time around;* which was why seemingly fatal mistakes were made. *This time,* on stage, the voice speaks, like that of another double. *Next time,* if all goes well, the voice will be that of a double successfully internalized: it will be the patient's own voice. It is a "He" that becomes a "Thou" and that ends up as an "I."

Obviously the most important single instrument in psychodramatic therapy is the director, and this is not just saying that the director is the psychiatrist: it is saying that he has to possess the specific talents required by the situations that arise on the psychodramatic stage.

4. If the "I" and "Thou" of life are modified in the psychodramatic theatre, so is the "They." The "They" of life is by definition general and amateur. The "They" of psychodrama is specialized and professional. At Dr. Moreno's public demonstrations the audience consists partly of those who see themselves as possible patients, partly of students of psychodrama. Any third element—such as the scoffers or the visitor who finds himself there by accident—is minor. So we are limited to people with a pre-established involvement, a curiosity that is really keen because it comes from need or greed.

It is perhaps seldom realized that in all theatrical situations there is a specific, understood relationship between actor and spectator, a kind of unwritten contract between the two. And it is probably just as seldom realized that the contract holds for only one type of theatre, while other types make other contracts. Thus what an expense-account executive at a Broadway show is buying from the actor is different from what, say, the Athenian people were buying from their festival players, which in turn was different from what Louis XIV had contracted for with Molière, and so on. A clear difference in aim, not to mention relationships outside the theatre, produces a clear difference in the actor/spectator relationship.

Such relationships, insofar as the facts are before us, can be examined in such terms as the degree of passivity (or its opposite) on the audience side. Lack of passivity can show itself in what I have just called need or greed: a felt need for what the spectacle intended to convey, an eagerness to know and in some sense possess it. At one extreme, audiences are both bored and bossy. "Entertain me," they say with a patronizing yawn. The actors are their slaves, their jesters, and will get whipped if they fail to be funny: what sharper whip than economic boycott? At the other end of the scale, the performer is looked up to: much is expected of him. The spectator is humble: it is he who hopes to profit by the exchange. The psychodramatic audience inclines to this other end of the scale, and its humility, combined as it is with neurotic involvement and intellectual curiosity, will show itself largely in the form of sympathy and human understanding.

It is not the audience's attitude in itself that is interesting but the way it functions in the reciprocal actor/spectator relationship. And it is necessary here to anticipate somewhat and say that one of the chief differences between drama and psychodrama is this: while drama is judged, fairly enough, by the effect the actor has on the audience, in psychodrama the highest priority goes to the effect the audience has on the actor. This effect, like that of the director's interventions, is by way of *propulsion*. The audience's sympathy oils the wheels; the audience's eager curiosity speeds things along. The whole occasion is a form of *public confession*. There is relief, and therefore pleasure, in such confession. The person who takes over much pleasure in it is called exhibitionistic. But if a degree of exhibitionism is normal, so is a degree of shyness. The presence of an audience makes it harder to be frank. Psychodrama addresses itself to this shyness and asks that it be tackled, not avoided, as it largely is by psychoanalysis.

5. A psychodramatic session differs from another two hours of living in that it is *literally* theatre while life is theatre only metaphorically speaking. I mean, to begin with, that there is a stage and that otherwise there is only an auditorium. This organization of space is so ruthlessly selective that most of the detail of actuality is omitted. To say the world is a stage is one thing. To represent the doings of this world *on* and *by* a stage is another. The physique of the psychodramatic theatre bears no resemblance to the world-in-general and not too close a resemblance to the world-in-particular. A scene in a garden will be redone without the garden. A scene about a man as a child will be redone without a child—the physical presence of a child— on stage. Conversely, the physical characteristics of *theatre*—a floor of a certain type, steps, suggestive bits of furniture, the spectators' seats arranged in a certain pattern, the rows of faces above the seats—have a quality (reality, atmosphere) of their own which contributes to the character of psychodrama as a whole.

The sheer physical nature of a theatre does more to determine the nature of the whole theatrical event than has commonly been appreciated, except by recent writers on environmental theatre who have gone to the opposite extreme. Yet, if we turn now to the psychodramatic event as a whole, there is one feature more decisive than environment, and that is—it is so obvious, one could forget to notice—re-enactment itself. Such and such was done in life: it will now be acted. Or, to return to the premise of role-playing, such and such was enacted in life: it will now be re-enacted. The first thing the director does is to ask the patient to *show* (instead of narrating) what once happened. Psychodrama is not life but recapitulation of life, living life over a second time, having your cake and eating it.

And this, which is indeed the key idea of psychiatry as we know it, can properly be the cue for a comparison of psychoanalysis with psychodrama. It was Freud who encouraged us to believe that, if anything at all could be done about our mental illnesses, it would be by going back to the time of their origin and reliving it. *The first time around,* we retreated at a certain point or stood still. The hope which therapy holds out is that, returning to this exact spot, we can *this time* make the needed advance from it. It is a repetition with a difference: an innovation, a nonrepetition.

All life is repetitious. There is the salutary and needed repetition by which good habits are formed. There is the baleful repetition by which bad habits are formed. There is the endless repetition of therapy sessions before the point is reached when any positive result is attained. Then, in the midst of repetition itself, the breakthrough. A paradox, if you will, and yet one which seems built into the process of living. Even love-making is all repetition—of words, of caresses, of body movement—until the breakthrough of orgasm. Scientists report similarly of the breakthrough into discovery; artistic performers of the breakthrough from the repetition of the rehearsal into performance.

As for bad habits, by innumerable repetitions an undesired action has become a habit. The habit is to be broken by yet another repetition, the repetition of perhaps the earliest performance, the original act, which is then *not* repeated, even once. It now leads when it should have led in the first place. In order to be freed from the old captivity one re-enters it one last time.

Now psychoanalytic therapy is itself psychodramatic—up to a

point. At one time, certainly, it specialized in the search for the early traumatic scene which was re-enacted, with the patient playing his childhood self and the analyst, for example, the hated father. Freud's first great discovery in the therapeutic sessions themselves was that the analyst did become father, mother, etc., in other words, that the patient assigned him roles—the main roles in his personal drama. Such *transference* was the key to the whole patient/doctor transaction, and therapy came about through the pain the patient endured in reliving the old troubles. If the patient fought back, he could hope to work through neurotic darkness into light.

It is unfortunately impossible to make any survey of the results of Freudian therapy and compare them with the results of any other therapy. One can only assert the a priori likelihood that one person might get more help from one form of therapy, another person from another. One can also point to what for many patients would be an unnecessary limitation in Freudian procedure. Freud in his day had to be much concerned with what one might term the sanctity of the confessional. His patients would never have "got it out" had anyone but the doctor been listening. Even at that they needed further encouragement by the device of the couch. You lie down and avoid looking the doctor in the eye. So in a way you are alone and can get into a reverie and say things you couldn't say into anyone's face. Freud preserves his patients from both the "Thou" and the "They." The patients' efforts to convert the analyst into a "Thou" are stoutly resisted. They are seen only as interference with the intention of making the latter a receptacle for roles not truly his, a ghost. "Look," the analyst must always be imagined as saying, "you have attributed to *me* all these characteristics of your father, but that's *your* problem."

Whatever help may be provided by such constantly re-enacted dramas of disenchantment, it may plausibly be maintained that there is often much to be gained by a contrary procedure: introducing the "Thou" by way of actor and the "They" by way of an audience and letting the analyst emerge into daylight as a director. That the director can then be accused of pushing things too much is inevitable, but this risk may be worth taking, and there are self-corrective elements, as noted above. The "Thou" of the psychodrama stage is neither the actual "Thou" nor a duplicate, but if he is a poor substitute in some ways, he is superior (as also noted) in others. The slow pain of free association, in conjunction with transference, produces certain realizations and has doubtless been curative on some occasions in some degree. But no patient is overly satisfied with the results, and that alone is justification for other methods than this Freudian one. And, as against transference, there is much to be said for engaging the other fellow, if not in his own person, at least in flesh-and-blood form. This encounter too inflicts a degree of salutary pain. And very painful indeed (as well as the opposite) is the presence of onlookers: something one has to face in life, something it may be needful to face in therapy. Many of us suffer specifically from fear of the others, and it may be doubted if psychoanalysis tackles this fear boldly enough. Many fear the flesh-and-blood actuality of the "Thou." It is often just this fear that makes a potential "Thou" into an actual "It." Here again, why not take the bull by the horns? There has been in the Freudian tradition itself a certain vestige of the Judaeo-Christian hatred of the body. In this respect Karl Kraus may have hit the mark when he said, "Psychoanalysis is the disease of which it purports to be the cure." And after all, Dr. Moreno is not the only one to ask if Freud hadn't overweighted things on the mental side in reaction against the physiological emphasis of nineteenth-century medicine. If today we talk in psychosomatic terms, by that token the somatic element is half of the whole. Is it not just as reasonable to get at the spirit through the body as vice versa? But these queries go beyond my topic, which is—to summarize this section—that, while there is drama between couch and chair in the dimly lit office, there is an ampler drama when "I" meets "Thou" upon a stage in the presence of a director and an audience.

III

If psychodramatic therapy is at a remove from life, dramatic art is at two removes from it, for while the protagonist of psychodrama is "spontaneous" and presents himself, the protagonist in

a play is held to a script on the basis of which he presents someone else.

If we see these two rearrangements of life—psychodrama and
drama—as running in competition with each other, which one
do we regard as the winner? It depends wholly on our own angle
of vision. The psychodramatist inevitably looks with horror upon
the written text. Dr. Moreno contemptuously terms it a "cultural
conserve," and sees it exclusively as a hindrance to spontaneity,
the highest value in his philosophy. From the viewpoint of
therapy, I believe his point is well taken. Here there is nothing
but advantage in improvisation. The protagonist is a patient, and
only his life matters. I have remarked that even the audience
in psychodrama exists for the sake of the protagonist, not vice
versa, as in drama. The dialogue, *a fortiori*, is all his. Even the
director is not an author but at best a sort of film-editor. Nor are
there any prescribed forms of dialogue or character, as with the
commedia dell'arte, which the psychodramatic "actor" must follow. Improvisation in any art—*commedia dell'arte* or a jazz
combo—is free only within narrow limits. By comparison, psychodrama offers its protagonist freedom indeed!

It is obviously possible that "confinement" within the rules of
an art may become a neurotic problem for a given individual.
Dr. Moreno reports that this was the case with John Barrymore.
This actor was sick (literally) of playing Shakespeare: he wanted,
he needed, to play Barrymore. Of course, one thing one would
need to know to make anything of this example would be whether
psychodramatic therapy, if diligently pursued, would have cured
Barrymore of alcoholism and whatever else ailed him. That he
wanted to play himself only proves him human: every infant
wants the same. But I am prepared to grant that subjection to
a written role may have compounded rather than solved this
particular man's problems. No written role was ever intended
to solve such problems anyway.

Spontaneity, as Dr. Moreno sees it, is a very useful, even an
inspiring idea. I would define it as one of the forms of human
freedom, a subjective form, in that it is a psychological, not a
political, one. It is a matter of how one feels. A spontaneous
man feels free. He feels disburdened of all the inhibitions and

evasions and shyness which normally hold him back from feeling what he could and would otherwise feel. If this is correct by way of definition, I would add that, like other forms of freedom, spontaneity operates within limits—within an iron ring of un-freedom, of unspontaneity. A completely free and spontaneous man would not only feel what he wants to feel but say what he wants to say—which would abolish politeness and saddle him with libel suits, to say the least. He would also do what he wants to—which would interfere grossly with the freedom of others. Life, then, has to set bounds to spontaneity. Indeed, some neurotic problems derive from such limits. Psychodrama moves the boundary posts out a little; but it doesn't throw them away.

What the psychodramatists have worked on, and worked for, is one particular kind of spontaneity which we may call solidifica-tion of the present moment. The neurotic's trouble is seen as the disintegration of the present: all is diffused into memories of the past and fantasies of the future. This entails great instability in the whole emotional system and, since joy is of the present, an incapacity for enjoyment: life is stale, flat and unprofitable. To re-create the present tense, to create spontaneity, is to bring a person back to life, it is to enable him to experience life in its fullness. For, as Blake put it,

> He who catches the joy as it flies
> Lives in eternity's sunrise.

If all this makes it sound as if the purpose of psychodrama were to stimulate to momentary pleasure I should go on to say, first, that this is no contemptible purpose but, second, that no one has claimed that a single achievement of that sort is a cure for any mental illness. Nor am I retracting the statement that psy-chodrama, like psychoanalysis, is painful: both therapies believe in possible progress through pain to pleasure. The difference between the two therapies, in regard to past and present, is that the Freudians keep constantly in mind the persistence of ancient hurts into the present and until recently have tried to refer the patient back just as constantly to the trauma of long ago, whereas the psychodramatist has always worked gradually back from the present. This labor, and not the discovery of trauma, is what "works through" the trouble: its pain, and not the vestigial pain of the trauma itself, is what the psychoanalyst assumes to be therapeutic. He begins "spontaneously" (i.e., as spontaneously as possible) in the present; works back to the obstacles, the rigidities, the nonspontaneities; only to help the patient back to the present; if he is lucky, with a true spontaneity.

Such a conception of spontaneity has in its favor that it is unpretentious. Its normal field of vision is a restricted one. Envisaged (initially at least) is not a whole life, a whole civilization, remade. In the clinical situation faced by the individual, doctor and patient can concentrate upon moment-to-moment experience. (If an invalid is still breathing, his breath will becloud a mirror.) Much psychiatry goes astray by overextending the field of vision: asking so many questions that there can be no coherent, compact answer. In psychodrama the question can usually be limited to: Is the patient's soul still breathing? Can this man warm up to an encounter with another man? Can he feel? Will his limbs go along with his feelings? Can he blush? Shout? Whisper? Kiss? Embrace? It is useful not to have to ask if a man is this or that type of neurotic, but instead: Is he in shape to survive as a human being among other human beings? Can he face the suffering? Can he experience the joy?

Limits are placed on spontaneity in life; in psychodrama; and in dramatic art. To the psychodramatic therapist the limits placed on spontaneity by art seem particularly threatening because, indeed, to impose a script and a role on someone would be to nip his psychodrama in the bud. This and the fact that psychodrama itself throws up scenes with considerable strength as dramatic *art* have encouraged Dr. Moreno to view the two activities as competitive and to feel that, in this competition, psychodrama wins. Actually, there is no competition. The problem, if it is a problem, is only that this therapy and this art overlap, and if chunks of a psychodramatic session are art, pure theatre could in some ways be therapeutic. More useful than taking sides, it seems to me, would be an attempt to sort things out a little.

To maintain flatly that theatre itself is or should be therapeutic will only lead us to the conclusion that it has less to offer than other therapies. If one had a serious mental illness, no amount of theatregoing in even the greatest of the theatres could be expected to help very much. Dr. Sophocles and Dr. Shakespeare would find themselves hopelessly unable to compete with Drs. Smith and Jones on Central Park West, neither of whom has ever laid claim to genius.

This is not to say that the notion of a *connection* between drama and therapy, between all the arts and therapy, is ill founded, only that it has been exaggerated, often by a kind of literal-mindedness. Take the most famous notion in the whole field: catharsis. There is a certain agreement, now, among scholars that the word should be taken as a medical term, that it signifies a purge, and not a moral purification as scholars used to think. Even so, there remains much to say, and chiefly that the word was pounced upon by psychiatrists of the 1890s and applied to a much lengthier and deeper process than any that a visit to a theatre could elicit. The word now described what happened in five years of psychoanalysis. Which, I would say, effectively takes it out of dramatic criticism altogether.

Was Aristotle wrong? Did he exaggerate? Did he mean something else? I doubt that a great pother is called for. After all, Aristotle said very little about catharsis, but the accepted modern interpretation of the word does not apply to many works of art, provided we can forget psychiatry for a moment and remember art for quite a few moments. Is it the case that a psychiatric session provides a thoroughgoing catharsis, whereas a play provides an inadequate one? To be sure, patients have often been known to vomit after a session; the theatre could seldom achieve such a result even if it tried.

What is needed, perhaps, is not that we judge art as therapy but that we distinguish one kind of therapy from another. Society needs therapy on two different scales. In the case of individual breakdowns, something more drastic than art—any art—is needed: that's why we have psychiatrists. But these complete breakdowns do not exhaust the list of psychic ills that flesh is heir to. At present, it is true, the others are just let go, if not actually encouraged, because they serve this or that sinister interest. Mother Nature does what she can. Many mental illnesses arise, take their course, and are gone, like physical illnesses. As Freud noted, there are even happy therapeutic accidents. But by and large, mental illness is left to flourish, is *encouraged* to flourish, as physical illness was in the Middle Ages. Which means both that individual therapy is needed by more and more people and that whole societies can be described as sick in something more than a metaphorical sense.

Now the arts are helpless in the face of such serious maladies. They can only help counteract such tendencies when other forces are doing so on a much larger scale than art itself: in other words when the situation is not as bad as all that. The Greeks viewed the arts as just a part of the good life, and the arts do need a good life to be part of, even if it's a good life that is beset by bad life. In such a context it makes sense to speak of a poet's "healing power" and even of the "corrective effect" of comedy. Poetry could not heal, and comedy could not correct, if things had gone more than just so far, *and not even then on their own.* But if there exists a real civilization, then, just as there are cures effected by nature, and others by lucky circumstances, so one could speak of the arts, too, as therapeutic, alongside other therapeautic agencies of a nonclinical sort. If it is a mistake to see art as standing alone, when it is in fact part of a common effort, a common culture, so it is a mistake to see art as therapy alone, when in fact, as we are all aware, it is other things as well.

What is the total function of art? That might seem too large a question to pose here, especially as there has never been any agreement on the answer. Yet there is no getting any further till the question *is* posed, and it is possible that the disagreements are not relevant. Suppose we just forge ahead.*

The function of art, say some, is to please. The function of art, say others, is to instruct. But what if being pleased is itself instructive? What if being instructed is itself a pleasure? The artistic impulse is the impulse to make something for fun. Why is it fun to make something?

The human creature has destructive urges. Little children wish to kill their parents. But destructive wishes trouble the conscience. We would like to atone for the sin of "thought crime." We would make restitution. We would repair the crockery we have broken,

---

* Not, of course, alone. In the following paragraphs I am drawing upon Shaw's Preface to *Misalliance* and two articles by the Scottish psychoanalyst, W. R. D. Fairbairn, "Prolegomena to a Psychology of Art" and "The Ultimate Basis of Aesthetic Experience," which appeared in volumes 28 and 29, respectively, of the *British Journal of Psychology.*

and restore it to its owner. The toy that a child willfully breaks but then guiltily repairs—or better still, replaces—and returns to its owner is perhaps the prototype of artwork. What arouses that "pity and terror" of which Aristotle spoke? Destruction and the resultant disorder. The tragic artwork is the poet's restoration of order and restitution for wrong. And his audience receives it as such. I offer these sentences only as thoughts that might help us understand the actual effect of tragedy, which is in part a healing effect, not indeed in the outright sense that tragedy would cure a case of epilepsy or schizophrenia, but in the sense that it springs from a need to feel that one can make good one's destructions. Without such feelings, I suggest, one would go mad. I am not saying that nothing but tragedy, or nothing but art, can provide them. I am saying that art, that tragedy, can provide them.

If the therapeutic element is only part of a whole, what is the whole? I'd suggest that the best name for the whole is *education*, though you may prefer, at one pole, *child-rearing* or, at the other, *culture*. I mean that art is the pabulum of the people, and that they should be nourished by it from childhood on: this (along with other contributions) makes a culture, makes up the spiritual life of a civilized community. The function of art is to educate, but to say so is not to plump for a didactic type of art: rather, for the idea that art per se is didactic, whereas what is called didactic art tends to fail to be didactic, fails actually to teach because it is boring and therefore soporific. It is because art is *fun* that it can succeed in being didactic, for there is no true teaching except in eagerness, amusement, delight, inspiration.

On the one side, then, all the deadly hate and destructiveness; on the other, the desire to make restitution by creating something for fun. Such restitution is therapeutic, among other things, not to the extent that it alone can clear up the acute sickness of either individuals or societies, but on a smaller scale which is nevertheless not all that small and which, in any case, is without time limit. Once there is a good society, even a society good enough to earn the name of civilization not chronically sick, art will join with Mother Nature and with Happy Accident, as also with other branches of culture, to attend to the psychopathology of everyday life, neutralizing many minor toxins, killing many small germs.

Which is but a modern and clinical way of restating the ancient belief that art is part of the good life.

Returning to the idea of spontaneity: if all spontaneity is a little unspontaneous too, as I believe, one can certainly find in art—and specifically in theatre—a kind of spontaneity. And indeed a true theatre person is one who craves this type of spontaneity. John Barrymore's problem, as I see it, was that he didn't want to be a theatre person, even though he had the talent for it: which is like being allergic to your own hormones.

Let me try to describe the spontaneity of an actor in a play. On the face of it he has surrendered it to the playwright: Barrymore mustn't be Barrymore, he must be Hamlet. But consider what really happens—from the first rehearsal on. At the first rehearsal, the actor hasn't yet built his characterization, so presumably what he brings along is himself and nothing but himself, and no script ever made an actor feel inhibited about this. As rehearsals progress a little, he comes into contact with his colleagues on stage. Maybe a little electricity is generated. He's attracted by the leading lady. He hates his male partner. Or vice versa. The electricity, in any case, is not between characters, it is between actors. Now the fondest hope of any professional actor (as of his director) is that the electricity generated in rehearsals will be preserved in the performance. That, to a large extent, is what rehearsals are for. Is such electricity a form of byplay, an additional stage effect like background noise? Just the opposite. Properly handled, it does not damage or distort the characterization itself, but is combined with it. Quite a trick! The characterization is to be what the author wanted: that, to be sure, is a principle of drama that there is no getting around. But the actor still meets the eye of another actor, not of a character, which is to say that both actors are still present: their own bodies and all that two human beings have that is not body. And they continue to use all of this, in live contact, as "I" and "Thou."

Should they fail to maintain the contact, could we say, "The actor having now withdrawn his own personality, what is left must be the character"? By no means: when the actors seem dead, as now they would, the characters would never be born. In other words, the life of the stage is a dual life, and through one of these two lives the principle of spontaneity enters, and is indeed essential: that the charatcer may *seem* to have a spontaneous existence, the actor must *actually* have a spontaneous existence. The pulling-off of this "trick"—it is of course much more—is perhaps the main task to which the actor addresses himself. Other things are important. There has to be a characterization to animate. But unless the actor animates it, a characterization has no theatrical value whatever. Conversely, if an actor comes on stage as his spontaneous self, and throws characterization to the winds, we may possibly get something of *psycho*dramatic interest—but even this not really, because the other actors won't relate to it properly, nor will we ourselves relate to it properly: it isn't what we "paid our money for." Whether we know it or not, we have different criteria for dramatic art, different expectations. Barrymore was finally ruined precisely by playing himself instead of the stage character. Life is life. Therapy is therapy. Drama is drama. All afford some freedoms, some opportunities for spontaneity, but, in all, freedom and spontaneity are very strictly circumscribed, so that the acceptance of the circumscription is as necessary an attitude to human beings as love of freedom. Freedom, says Engels, is the recognition of necessity. Goethe says, *"In der Beschraenking zeigt sich erst der Meister"*—"Only in his confrontation of limits does a master show his mettle." This is another way of saying: we marvel that spontaneity exists at all; and we marvel how much spontaneity can be created by masters of living, of therapy, or of art.

Walt Anderson

———•———

Dance Therapy

Next to psychodrama, dance is probably the most widely used form of art therapy. Like psychodrama, it links emotions with physical movements and is a more active experience than most traditional forms of therapy.

> The art of dancing stands at the source of all the arts that express themselves first in the human person. . . .
>   Dancing is the loftiest, the most moving, the most beautiful of the arts, because it is no mere translation or abstraction from life; it is life itself.
>
> —HAVELOCK ELLIS

I find it a kind of reassuring thought, in these morose times, that at any given moment a sizable portion of the human race is dancing. Consider the incredible variety of dances that people do: rain dances, war dances, dervish twirls, flamenco, the waltz, square dances, all those ethnic numbers you see at folk festivals, the twist and all its progeny, plain old cheek-to-cheek.

Then picture this scene: I am in a small upstairs room in a psychiataric clinic with five other people: a dance therapist, a young doctor and three autistic children. We all have our shoes off, and we are dancing. From a record player comes the sound of rock music—it's Jimmy Cliff singing "You Can Get It if You Really Want"—and each of the children takes a turn being the

SOURCE: This essay originally appeared as "Pas de Psyche" in *Human Behavior*, March 1975, pp. 56–60. Copyright © 1975 *Human Behavior* Magazine. Reprinted by permission.

leader. One marches around the circle clapping hands, we all march around the circle clapping hands. Another sits down and pounds the floor, we all sit down and pound the floor. Sometimes the children leave the circle physically or disappear inside themselves, and there are other moments when we are all together, moving with harmony and flow.

For the children, day-care patients at the clinic, the session is a routine part of their afternoon's activities. For me, it is a glimpse into one corner of the world of dance therapy.

Dance therapy—why not? Aren't all the patterns that we develop as we grow up—the phenomena we later learn to call neuroses or some such *mental* term—also physical patterns that can logically be dealt with in physical ways? Wilhelm Reich thought so, back in the '20s, and his mode of therapy changed accordingly from conventional verbal psychoanalysis to massage and breathing exercises. A lot more people think so today, and the new body therapies are everywhere: Reichian and Neo-Reichian schools such as Rolfing and bioenergetics, Gestalt therapy with its heavy emphasis on physical awareness, the encounter-group movement with its "bodymind" techniques. Dance, which expresses the whole eloquent range of human physical movement, has a natural place in all of this, and the field of dance therapy is growing (as one therapist described it to me) by leaps and bounds.

Dance therapy is not exactly new. Its use in this country dates back to around 1940, and dance may in fact be one of the oldest kinds of therapy in existence. Among primitive people, dance rituals are commonly used as cures for the ills of body and soul; dancing was probably therapy several thousand years before it became show business and the job of healing was handed over to the people who believed that the way to cure anxiety was to have the patient lie very still on a couch and talk about it.

Nevertheless, dance therapy has the feel of a new and still-formative discipline—the American Dance Therapy Association was founded in 1966, and as of this writing there are only four colleges that have graduate programs for dance therapy students: UCLA, Texas Women's University, Hunter College and NYU. The profession is just getting official recognition from civil service bureaus, and most of the dance therapy programs in half-way houses, rehabilitation centers and day-care clinics have begun only in the past few years. Another new development is the growing number of dance or movement therapists who do not work through institutions at all but, rather, maintain private practices—dealing either with people who are in some other kind of therapy and doing dance work as a supplement to that, or with people who are in dance therapy only.

The basic idea of dance therapy is that body movement is a natural medium of self-expression and communication—a capacity that becomes impaired, to some extent, in all of us—and that an expanded ability to move the body can also be an expansion and reintegration of the whole personality. Dance therapy also has a heavily *social* orientation: there are a few movement therapists who work with patients on a one-to-one basis, but probably 95 percent of the work being done in this field is group activity. Sometimes dancing creates a sense of group cohesiveness far more effectively than any amount of talking.

For several months, I attended weekly dance therapy sessions, and the experience showed me how true this is. The group was made up of about a dozen people: students and people in therapy —I never knew exactly who was which—and we developed a real feeling of friendliness and cooperation that was based entirely on our dancing together. We rarely talked, and there was not much socializing outside the meetings. As our sense of conviviality grew, somebody in the group proposed having a party and the group leader discouraged it. She said that we would just fall back into our social roles and verbal routines and thus lose some of our ability to communicate to each other without words. I think she was right.

Dancing does communicate. If a person is creating a spontaneous dance movement and you watch it closely—or, better yet, attempt to copy it—you begin to pick up in your own body some of the feelings being experienced by the dancer. One dance therapy exercise based on this premise is a dream or memory enactment done in groups of four: each person does a dance that acts out his or her own dream or memory, while the other three follow it and copy it with their own motions. There is no prior discussion of what the dance will be about, and after it is over the three followers report what happened to them during the

dance. The first time I participated in this exercise I chose a
memory—recent and vivid in my mind at the time—of something
that had happened to me on an outing. Returning alone from
an easy hike to the top of a mountain, I had suddenly found
myself on a steep slope of loose dirt and rocks, with no trail and
a rocky river gorge several hundred feet below me. It was a
dangerous and scary spot, and as I worked my way out of it, I
had felt a knot of fear in my gut and had even slipped into fantasies of somebody telling my wife and son that I had been killed.
So I danced this memory, as best I could on a solid and level
space. And when it was over the first person who had been following me, a woman, sat down breathlessly on the floor, reported
feelings of fear and nausea, and told us she suffered from acro-
phobia. It communicates.

Another thing I found out about dance therapy during these
sessions was that it feels good. I would come out feeling loose,
happy and full of energy, and the glow always stayed with me for
several days. The curious facet was that, although the sessions
involved a lot of strenuous physical activity, I came out of them
feeling more energetic than I had before. Actually, there is nothing curious about that at all; maintaining physical tension is
hard work, and letting go of it feels good. Elizabeth Rosen's
book *Dance in Psychotherapy* puts it this way:

> Persistent hypertonus of muscles has been recognized as one of the
> symptoms of anxiety, the physical reaction of the body to emotional
> disturbance. In psychotic patients this psychophysical phenomenon
> shows itself in two rather distinctive patterns. In the hyperactive
> patient, excessive activity, restlessness, ticks, and a variety of in-
> voluntary grimaces have been described as one kind of response
> to tension. On the other hand, static rigidity of the body, in-
> flexibility of joint action, and postural distortions are equally
> common reactions. In both extremes unrelieved accumulated ten-
> sion acts to disturb the normal rhythmic functioning of the body
> which is based on an alternation between relaxation and con-
> traction. Inevitably, the physical effects of continued hypertonus
> result in exhaustion.

What all this means is that the patient—and you can take that
term to include us all—is *tired,* and that the tiredness comes
not so much from burning energy as from blocking it within

the body or channeling it into stale repetitive patterns of movement.

We all have limited repertoires of movement. Stop for a moment and think of anybody you know, and then picture some
of the movements characteristic of that person. Then picture some
of the movements that person would *not* make. Quickly you begin
to get a sense of that person's physical personality, the movements that are part of it and the movements that are beyond the
boundaries.

One of the aims of dance therapy is to stretch those boundaries, on the belief that an expanded ability to move is an expanded ability to *be*. This is especially important in some of the
newer uses of dance therapy—such as with blind people, who
tend to develop movement habits called "blindisms"; with the
aged and the physically handicapped; with people recovering
from operations or serious accidents. One dance therapist told
me she has developed a whole repertoire of dance movements
for people who cannot walk.

The aim of expanding body-movement range—vocabulary,
some dance therapists call it—is also a major focus of the work
being done in mental institutions. One of the characteristics
of most inmates of such places—in fact, one of the main reasons
they *become* inmates—is the prevalence of obviously limited
patterns of body action. In any psychiatric ward, you will see
ritual movements endlessly repeated or stonelike immobility or
—less conspicuous but equally important—signs of loss of awareness of parts of the body. The dance therapist's task is to create
unthreatening opportunities for people to move in new and satisfying ways, to rediscover their own bodies.

In dance, as in other forms of therapy, the process can be
guided either by the therapist or by the patient. One therapist
described to me her approach to one-to-one work in terms that
closely resembled Gestalt therapy: the emphasis was on getting
in touch with what goes on inside and then finding ways to express it; the work began not with music and movement but with
attention to the here-and-now inner state of the client. Other
therapists guide the work with "challenges" that are put in the
form of questions, asking patients to find new ways of moving
different parts of the body. Any dance therapist must develop a

heightened ability to observe the ways people move, and some use an "effort-shape" notation system by which movement repertoires can be recorded and kept on file so that changes can be systematically observed and one dance therapist can communicate more clearly to another about her work with specific patients. (I use feminine by preference here for the simple reason that nearly all dance therapists are women.)

In a group, the therapist may act as leader, taking the members together through a sequence that begins with simple warm-up movements and gradually gets the entire body in motion. Such a sequence usually involves not only movement of one's own body but interactions with props—many dance therapists use a variety of them, to give patients new experiences of feeling and moving objects of different size, shape and texture—and interactions with other people. This is a delicate area. Many patients are afraid of physical contact, and so are a lot of the people who run mental institutions. But the dance therapists I have talked to generally agree on its value and manage to skillfully lead their groups into various kinds of physical contact such as hand holding, back rubbing, even massaging.

As I participated in some dance therapy sessions, it became apparent to me that the patients were discovering for themselves what I had learned about dance therapy: that it's fun. And I also began to see how important this is. In my research—reading books and papers about dance therapy—I had been searching for insight into how, and how well, it works, what there is about music and motion that helps people to change, integrate themselves, expand their abilities to communicate and move. I had been trying to understand what it does, and then one day, in the recreation room of a big city hospital's psychiatric ward, I saw a bunch of patients dancing and laughing and I realized that a big part of the truth was right there before me.

Just before the dance therapy I had sat in on a briefing where the staff went over the records on the patients who would be coming to the session that day. The records carried a heavy load of personal tragedies: drug addiction, alcoholism, self-mutilation (one man had cut off one of his own testicles with a jackknife), attempted suicide. Then, fifteen minutes or so later, we were all in a room with the same patients, bouncing around in a circle within a length of elastic rope, having a tug of war, making animal noises—and people were laughing. Not everybody. Some of the patients sat on the sidelines and watched, some participated with a good deal of reserve or inhibition. But, still, most of the people in the group were actually having a good time, and laughing. Now laughter—especially that kind of laughter, the sound of people having fun—is a very rare sound to hear in a mental institution. So many tools that go by the name of therapy either deaden consciousness—drugs, neurosurgery—or actually cause pain—shock treatments, all the armory of behavior-shaping negative reinforcements—that it seemed really important to me to see a form of therapy that was not merely justified as helping the patients to find happiness at some vague future point in their lives but was itself an immediate source of joy.

Perhaps for this very reason, dance therapy is not really taken seriously by most of the psychiatrists, psychologists and bureaucrats who people the upper levels of the mental health establishment. It is *accepted*—the number of organizations that include dance or movement therapy in their programs is increasing rapidly—but that is not quite the same thing as being taken seriously and understood. Dance therapy in most institutions is connected with occupational and recreational therapy and functions at a fairly low level of the therapeutic totem pole; it is a pastime for the inmates. Dance therapists are mostly dedicated, and underpaid, young women. Their training includes courses in psychological theory, but the training of psychotherapists rarely includes any exposure to dance or body-movement techniques. I have heard of a few clinical psychologists who call themselves dance therapists; no psychiatrists. Most psychotherapy operates above the neckline.

I suspect this is going to change. There is a lot of innovation going on among the various mental health professions these days. I mentioned a few of the many new body-oriented forms of psychotherapy that are already beginning to have an impact on the traditional "talk" therapies; these tend to be associated with humanistic theories of the optimum development of the whole person and also with the general idea of therapy as closely allied to (if not one of) the arts. If all these factors can be woven together and absorbed into the mainstream of psychotherapy, it might mean a new valuing of free, integrated and creative people—and also the development of some new and workable ways of growing in such directions. If you look at it that way, it seems like a hopeful and noble enterprise, and a dance well worth joining.

The Torta

1412 Central SE

Jazz — $1.00 door charge

8:00

The Torta
Old World Coffee House
& Garden Cafe

BBY
OSPITAL CENTER
919
ANNA KASEMAN HOSPITAL
, NEW MEXICO

CUMULATIVE REPORT   PG 1
1548 HR   8/20/1979
ROOM: 401B   NS:400
DR: DEMPSY

H E M O G R A M ****************************

MCV	MCHC		
80-100	31.5-		
	36.5		
U3	%		
88	34.6		
89	34.8		

R E N T I A L ****************************

ONCYTE	EOSIN	BASOPHL	PLT EST
P TO 6	UP TO 5	UP TO 2	
%	%	%	
4	0	0	ADEQ
2	0	0	ADEQ

R F H O L O G Y ****************************

POLYCHR	POIK	REMARK	
0	0	0	

Erma Dosamantes Alperson

Nonverbal and Verbal Integration

*Again and again the subject of integration arises: integration of therapy
with the arts, integration of the person, integration of new approaches
with old ones. The author of this essay—who is a movement therapist,
dancer, and clinical psychologist—deals with integration of movement
and verbalization. This can be taken as another expression of Koestler's*
reculer pour mieux sauter *theme: movement takes the person into
deeper levels of existence, and then verbalization builds whatever has
been discovered there into the known and communicable personality.*

Historically, a therapist's role, goals, and techniques have in part
been influenced by the dominant cultural views of the day regarding the nature of man and of woman and their relationship
to their environment.

At present, we are witnessing the confrontation between two
ideologically opposing cultural forces, each of which is reflected
in the views of the adherents of the various therapeutic camps of
today.

On the one hand, we have the older, more established ideology
born out of a culture that prizes pragmatic-materialistic values.
This perspective stresses mankind's "functional" value to its society. From this vantage point, it becomes desirable for a person
to be rational, in control of her emotions and her body, and to

SOURCE: Presented at the Second California Regional Conference of the
American Dance Thearapy Association, Santa Barbara, June 1–3,
1973. Copyright © 1977 by Erma Dosamantes Alperson. Printed by
permission of the author.

adjust or attempt to fit herself into her world as it exists, causing minimal threat or upset among those around her.

Dance from this perspective is regarded as a form of entertainment that only an elite may be privy to perform and enjoy.

In the early fifties and sixties, a rebellious voice began to emerge from a small group of psychologists and psychiatrists—namely, Maslow, Rogers, Gendlin, Perls, Szasz, and Laing—to challenge this functional ideology, suggesting that mankind's potential for self-directed creative behavior was being stymied; that human beings were only partially educated and only partly functioning entities by virtue of having lost contact with the less rational, more intuitive aspects of their experiencing.

Much of the literature originating from this latter group has become part of the heritage of the humanist movement; the thinking of this movement has influenced and in turn been influenced by creative artists who view art and dance as powerful media for increasing self-awareness through contact with nonverbal aspects of our experience.

As a force, this humanist orientation attacks the dominant condition of our time—our obsession with control, analysis, and technological rationality.[1] The therapeutic techniques that have emerged from this perspective have tended to stress nonverbal modes of communication; they prefer touch to therapeutic distance; they focus more on sensation than on analysis and stress phenomenological observation over theoretical explanation.

Both functional and humanist camps have extreme adherents for their viewpoint. On the one extreme, we see therapists who would exclude the somatic and the erotic; on the other extreme, those who would exclude language because it represents some aspect of our rational selves.

It seems to me that if our goals as therapists are to achieve greater vitality, increased self-awareness, and integration or wholeness within ourselves, as well as a sense of effectiveness in relating to our world, we must look for the best possible means to help our clients synthesize two modes of human consciousness:

1. Bernard Gunther, "Sensory Awakening and Relaxation," in *Ways of Growth*, ed. Herbert A. Otto and John Mann (New York: The Viking Press, 1968), pp. 60–68; Sam Keen, "Sing the Body Electric," *Psychology Today*, October 1970, p. 56.

the rational with the intuitive or the verbal with the preverbal.

Gendlin, who has done much research on the phenomenological experiencing process (another name for this process is our "ongoing subjective experience") , describes two distinct levels of this process: the felt level and the symbolic level.[2] Ornstein claims a physiological basis for this distinction but refers to these two kinds of experiencing as two unique types of human consciousness: the intuitive and the rational.[3]

Because ours is a culture that exalts the rational-cognitive side of our nature while it disparages the physical emotional side, most of us soon learn to regard the world from a primarily intellectual perspective.[4] The consequence of this partial training is that when we become strongly aroused, we respond in either constricted or vague, undifferentiated ways; lacking familiarity with our affective-motor systems, we also lack control over our bodies and bodily derived emotional responses.

The problem with most verbal therapies of today that aim to promote personal growth and change is that they exclude almost totally the bodily derived felt-level of experiencing; they also have failed to recognize that the felt level must precede the conceptual level if the person is not to remain cut off from her kinesthetic-affective reactions. The act of verbalizing our experience often serves to alienate us further from our experiential body process, for it causes one to adopt the role of an observer looking at one's self, rather than being the active participant-creator of one's own experience.

A body-sense dissociation afflicts almost everyone in our culture with the exception of those exceptional creative artists and scientists who can move freely between the two modes of human consciousness and tap both in producing their original works.

Movement therapy that is process-oriented and works toward sensitizing the person to her felt-level experiencing through move-

2. Eugene T. Gendlin, *Experiencing and the Creation of Meaning* (New York: The Free Press of Glencoe, 1962); *idem*, "Focusing," *Psychotherapy: Theory, Research and Practice* 6 (1969) , pp. 4–15.

3. Robert E. Ornstein, *The Psychology of Consciousness* (New York: The Viking Press, 1973) .

4. Albert Mehrabian, *Nonverbal Commuunication* (Chicago: Aldine Publishing Co., 1972) .

ment, and allows the person contact with the flow of emergent
emotional states, images, ideas, and verbalization, provides the
most natural sequence for integrating both levels of the experiencing process, the felt and the symbolized.[5]

Therapists who begin with the body and body movement and
work outward to include conceptualization adopt an inside-
looking-out approach to the study of human experiencing. This
approach makes the person the central source of her own experiential process. In therapy, the person becomes engaged in a self-
discovering process: discovering what her experience is, as it
unfolds in her awareness. The function of the therapist becomes
that of a facilitator, helping to enhance the person's optimal
contact with the entirety of her own experiental process.[6]

I believe that the unique contribution of an authentic movement experience within the context of a movement therapy
session is that:

1. It can acquaint the person *with herself as the source of her
   felt-experiencing process.*
2. It puts the person in touch with *what her actual felt-expe-
   ience is.*
3. It allows the person an opportunity to *express outwardly
   the intent of her actions, in a safe, nonexplicit way.*

I oppose the view that would have movement therapists re-
strict themselves to the movement aspect alone, since the integrative aspect of synthesizing movement with conceptualization
would be lost; and all politics notwithstanding, the totality of
the experiencing process not only includes how we perceive the
world and how we react to what we perceive, but also encom-
passes our *attempts to relate and share our experience with others.*
To have an effective impact on others, we need to relate verbally
with them.

I believe that the verbalization that flows from the movement
experience can enhance and extend the person's felt experiencing
outward. Before talking about the contribution that verbalization

5. Erma Dosamantes Alpersom, "Carrying Experiencing Forward through
Authentic Body Movement," *Psychotherapy: Theory, Research and Practice*
11 (1974), pp. 211–214.
6. Harold Rugg, *Imagination* (New York: Harper & Row, 1963).

can make to the movement experience, I would like to draw distinction between two kinds of client verbalization.

Just as there are inauthentic and authentic kinds of movement, there are inauthentic and authentic kinds of verbalization. Inauthentic verbalization is "abstract verbalization"; the verbal statement made by the person is not connected with her felt experience. We see it most clearly when the client's statements are contradicted by her gestures, postures, and voices. In such instances, the lack of congruence between two modes of communication, the verbal and the nonverbal, becomes quite obvious. *Speech that is not congruent with the person's felt-level experience is abstract speech.*

The usage of language itself also will often reveal whether or not the person is in touch with or cut off from her felt experiencing. For example, if in the process of talking I switch from talking about myself as "I" and begin referring to myself in the neutral "one" or "it," I am essentially disclaiming myself as the source of my own experience; I am distancing myself from it.

The degree of being cut off from my felt experiencing will reflect itself in my usage of language. The most extreme kind of cutting off is exhibited in the person who has to distance herself from her felt experiencing to the greatest degree (e.g., the person who hears voices ordering her to hit the therapist reflects, in her indirectness, the fact that she cannot claim her own feelings and actions and must project responsibility for them onto an external source, namely, her voices).

Another example of the way that language reveals our contact or lack of it with our experiential felt process is the tense in which we cast our verbal statements. If, as I am talking, I begin to talk about my past, I am essentially distancing myself from my felt experiencing by adopting the role of an observer seeing myself in the then; I may be feeling so uncomfortable by an ongoing present experience that I begin to run away from it and escape into a past, already finished situation.

In contrast to abstract or incongruent speech, there is a kind of verbalization that is congruent with one's felt experiencing. I call this kind of verbalization "felt verbalization" to indicate its congruence with felt experiencing.

This kind of verbalization is characterized by a high degree of *intensity* (or involvement) and a high degree of *directness* between the speaker and the person she is addressing.[7]

It is an interesting phenomenon that the person who moves authentically may not also be able to verbalize authentically; the reverse is also true. However, I believe, as Ornstein does, that the truly integrated person can do both with equal facility.

When felt verbalization follows an authentic movement experience, an additional experiential component is added: that of making explicit our felt reactions toward others and our world.

In the interpersonal context of a movement therapy session, the contribution of felt verbalization will exhibit itself in the following ways:

1. *One's feelings are validated in the presence of another.* Whether in the context of a group or in the context of a one-to-one therapeutic relationship, hearing someone confirm some feeling or experience you have not previously shared helps to validate your existence as a fellow human being, which in turn allows you to feel less alienated from yourself and others.

2. *The wording* of the content of what the person is talking about *is less important than the sharing aspect of the experience.* Thus, while the person can give multiple kinds of statements to the same felt movement event, all of which would satisfy the person equally well in describing the experience, the more crucial aspect in promoting change in perception and behavior is the sharing of the experience, with all the feelings connected with it. An atmosphere of intimacy, trust, and caring develops when the person perceives herself empathically understood by another, which in turn can give her the courage to explore herself further.

3. *In becoming explicit through verbalization, one seeks clarification of ambivalent feelings and perceptions experienced while moving with another.* The act of verbalizing mixed attitudes and feelings toward another allows the person an opportunity to hear her own confusion and get useful feedback from the other person.

4. *Verbalization is riskier and less safe than moving with an-*

7. Mehrabian, *Nonverbal Communication.*

other, particularly with regard to the expression of feelings that are taboo in our culture (such as strong, aggressive, or sexual feelings); *however, making feelings and intentions explicit can lead to owning up to one's reactions and taking responsibility for them.* When an individual can make explicit her reactions toward others, it is inevitable that some of these reactions will be of a negative nature. To acknowledge these reactions in the presence of others is risky because the person cannot disguise her hostile intent nor can she know in advance how her remarks will be received by others. She may be rejected. Yet this very act of claiming what one feels leads to what Perls calls "maturation" or the ability to stand on one's own two feet and assume responsibility for one's actions and feelings.[8]

I have not exhausted the ways that felt verbalization can lead to further personal change within an interpersonal context; however, from the ones I have already mentioned, you can gather some cue as to the attitude I believe ought to be adopted by the facilitator in relation to her clients' verbalizations subsequent to a movement experience:

1. The facilitator, I believe, should provide the climate as well as the opportunity for her client to make whatever comments she wishes to make to her movement experience.
2. This means that she must not press the person to make herself explicit, but must be willing to wait until the client chooses to talk. If the client chooses not to explicate herself, the therapist must respect that position. For it is only when the person feels safe and secure in the relationship that she will risk making herself explicit.
3. The therapist's own verbal responses to the client's verbal statements will be valid only to the degree to which they reflect accurately and empathically a genuine understanding of what the person herself is saying. For when the client feels herself accurately and empathically understood, she will continue to stay with her own felt process and continue to explore it further.

8. Frederick S. Perls, *Gestalt Therapy Verbatim* (Lafayette, Calif.: Real People Press, 1969).

4. The facilitator should function to maintain the client's focus on her own experience and not get abstracted or indirect. When that is no longer possible, it is a sign to the therapist that the person is no longer speaking from her felt experiencing; therefore it is time to go back to movement and put the client back in touch with herself and her felt level of experiencing once more.

In summary, I believe that a synthesis of authentic movement and authentic verbalization allows the person the greatest contact with the entirety of her own experiential process.

Frederick Wells

Psychosonics

Various activities that go by the name of music therapy are commonly found in psychiatric institutions, but in fact music—like dance—is rarely understood or taken seriously by psychotherapists. Frederick Wells, music therapist and Chairman of the Division of Creative and Performing Arts at Lone Mountain College in San Francisco, is developing a new approach that involves a much greater respect for the power of sound to influence human emotions.

In the early 1960s a great deal of attention and enthusiasm centered on the symphonic works of Gustav Mahler, a late romantic whose works had never been fully understood or appreciated in his own time. In response to this interest I offered a class to study Mahler's complete works. Early in the course I found I needed new techniques to put listeners in touch with his highly personalized and emotional style. The procedures I employed occurred to me intuitively during each week's class. This was a significant contrast to my usual manner of teaching, in which the classroom hours were spent communicating material carefully predetermined outside of class.

The response to these methods was different from what I had expected. Instead of putting the class in better understanding of Mahler, it put them in deeper touch with themselves by way of Mahler's music. I found that the real material of the course was the individuals in the class. From the techniques we were using,

SOURCE: This essay was written for this volume. Copyright © 1977 by Frederick Wells. Printed by permission of the author.

individuals began experiencing feelings ranging from depression and anxiety to ecstasy and joy. More than mere listeners of Mahler, we had become experiencers of Mahler's own emotional states, which were, in one way or another, our own.

With so much emotional catharsis occurring in the class I found I needed every tool of psychological training I had received. My role was broadened from a teacher of music history to what I assumed was a music therapist, or a therapist using music.

After this initial experience I designed other courses and workshops with such titles as "Music and Personal Creativity" and "Exploring the Self through Music." What happened in these groups reaffirmed my own theories about the role music might perform in therapy.

Music Therapy

During my years of schooling I had spent an internship at a California state mental hospital. On the hospital staff was a music therapist whose primary role was to create occupation and diversion. In fact when music therapists are promoted to a higher position they assume the new title of "Recreation Director"! I knew from my experience as a therapist on the wards and in attendance at staff meetings that the music therapist shared no real part in the conscious effort of dealing with mental illness. The use of music was a form of recreation in which patients performed at levels and in manners similar to those of elementary school pupils.

Could this be all there was to music therapy? Further investigation showed that although there were degrees in music therapy, journals of music therapy, and a professional society of music therapists, there was no integration of *psychological* therapy into the musician's work. Most of the material available seemed to show no assimilation of the psychological techniques of the past decade. Preoccupation with pseudoscience, testing, and proving games had assembled a pile of tables and statistics about hearing tones and identifying moods. But no practical work had been reported that used music's symbolic forms to reach the human being.

Most psychological practitioners are skeptical of any but verbal methods of treatment. There is still some suspicion that art therapies, body work, and diet control have little to do with improving the mental-emotional complex. Talking-it-out has long been the only accepted form of work. Recently, however, role playing, psychodrama, bioenergetics, megavitamin therapy, and Gestalt have all entered the scene and have shown significant healing contributions. Therapies using art, dance, drama, and music are being given new opportunity to contribute through these recent newer approaches.

Effect of Music

Viewing music as mere entertainment or diversion, with no effect on the listener, is a modern misconception. We know that in ancient Greece and Egypt music was thought to have influence over the emotional and moral character of the person. Exactly how this was so is not clearly known to us. In Greece, the different modes or scales were thought to create different moods in the listener. This would indicate a very sophisticated level of listening awareness and presumably musical training. Of course, the ancient world was free of the continual sound pollution that penetrates our ears and minds. We hear music while shopping, while eating, while studying, in cars and airplanes, in doctors' and dentists' offices, from the neighborhood rock band, and as background to conversation. Compounded with this is the daily bombardment of noise from traffic, airplanes, motors, construction, and household clatter. It's no small wonder that we have lost the ability to hear more than the mere outline of musical designs. In a world where the only sounds were that of wind and water, animals and voices, any artificially produced tones would command great attention. Nor was music a continual happening, so that one might wait for very special occasions to hear music at all.

In medieval times, Western modes were thought to convey specific affects: Mode I—somberness, Mode II—sadness, Mode III—mystery, etc. The concept that music could provoke certain specific feelings, resulting from its tonal structure, continued into the Renaissance and Baroque periods. The primary element to be heard was the relationship of tones, especially the placement of the semitone. But the sophisticated listening of those times is not present today except for a small group of highly trained musicians.

The main point here is that music has always been understood to have some effect on human feeling. That alone would be significant if we believe that the basic nature of any organism is feeling—for example, as Whitehead's philosophy proposes. It is the human organism's feelings that give rise to emotions. The emotions are an expression of the state of the person's feelings. Thus, if music can stimulate feeling, it may have an influence on emotion and the person's total well-being.

It is a popular misconception that music contains feelings. When we say "that song is so tragic" or "that is such a happy piece," we are actually projecting into the music our own moods. Patterns of sound are nothing more than the variations in frequency, amplitude, overtone, and combinations of these physical occurrences. It is the mind that interprets such stimuli with feelings.

This character of music, which makes it a receptive image for our feelings, lends to music its greatest power. Unlike the other arts, music has few connections with the given conditions of the natural world. While the visual arts employ colors and lines of the natural world, very little music reminds us of anything we've ever heard in nature. Even the most abstract paintings contain colors, lines, and patterns from visual experience. But Beethoven's *Pastoral* Symphony contains no sounds of nature, for where in nature can be found an F-major scale in well-tempered tuning? Or where have we ever heard violins, horns, guitars, or organs in the natural creation?

Such sounds and the organization of these sounds into forms we call music are created in the human mind. Music has formally been understood as the most abstract of all the arts. It is like nothing other than itself. In the nineteenth century, music was esteemed as the greatest of the arts, by poets and painters alike. And in the medieval universities it was one of the quadrivium taught—the others being mathematics, geometry, and astronomy. Somehow, humanity has created an abstract experience with enormous power to command attention and awe and to invoke in us the experience of feelings and moods.

With such potential, music commands significant possibilities as a therapeutic agent far outreaching its traditional recreational and occupational roles. Realizing that, I have been developing a therapeutic approach that I call *psychosonics*. My purpose in coining the term is to prevent confusion and false expectations in those who know the traditional music-therapist approach. The term also allows for a broader definition of music to include any source of sound that we hear with attraction, awareness, empathy, and response.

Psychosonics

At the outset it must be stated that the mere presence of music in someone's life does not include the presence of mental health. Nor does the degree of attention and awareness to musical material bring about an increase in humanizing effects. The past couple of centuries have been filled with musicians who have been mentally ill, depressed, neurotic, or attached to drug use. Music alone is no magic for changing the human condition (although it has at times had an effect on the social condition). Used, however, in connection with psychotherapeutic work it can become a useful adjunct to the healing process.

In seeking to use music therapeutically, one assumes a goal. Therapy implies a need for change or growth in a particular direction. Since not all therapists are agreed on that goal, I shall state my own particular bias. Adjustment and control as goals for human behavior always contain some social and political presuppositions that form the framework for therapies oriented in those directions. Our present Western society has produced a framework that both promises and inhibits individualization processes. Adjustment to this ambiguity has produced violence and passivity at both psychological and physical levels.

Hence the goal of therapy becomes self-fulfillment or self-actualization rather than adjustment or control. And in arriving at self-actualization one may have to deal first with psychotic and neurotic mental structures. But regardless of how many side trips are necessary, the goal remains defined as becoming centered, whole, open, accepting, truthful, aware, mindful, and capable of giving and receiving love. By such a definition, most persons would be considered less than fully realized beings. But the fact of present conditions does not preclude potential fulfillment. Therapy, then, is the development of those conditions as the ground from which the person participates with the environment of events in time and space.

Other ways of describing this state exist. One popular way in therapy today is the experiencing of the "here and now" without the constraints of guilt-producing memory or anxiety-producing projection. There is also a strong relationship between this type of goal and those of sensory awareness and meditation. But whatever the approach, the goal remains to authenticate the self rather than to adjust or control it.

How music can contribute to attaining that goal is the subject of the remainder of this discussion. And the first detail that must be understood is what is meant by the term "music." Avantgarde composers and would-be rock stars alike have had to respond to the question: "You call that music?" My answer to that question is yes—and perhaps a lot more than is likely to be considered music can become music. Categorical prejudice is the manner in which taste is expressed. Someone may find that rock music arouses nervousness and anxiety, while classics bring about feelings of calmness and strength. Another person reports that classical music always sounds depressing, whereas rock "turns him on." So it goes with taste. But the therapist goes beyond the influences of taste. Every type of feeling, negative or positive, becomes an opportunity for exploration.

As an adjunctive tool for the therapist, music can help accomplish certain specific effects. These may be musically induced physical changes in breathing, pulse, and facial and muscular tensions. Or the effects may be experienced in mental changes, in attention, sensing, and awareness. Finally, music can become an effective affect-projector in working with unconscious levels, memory recall, associations, depression-expression polarity, fantasy, roles, and self-images.

The success of the employment of music for therapeutic goals depends to a large part on the therapist's possessing a variety of psychological skills combined with a very intensive and broad listening spectrum in the field of music. A practitioner of psychosonics will be like a prescribing pharmacist of sound, having an intimate acquaintance with all the types and styles of music and intuitive understanding of when and how they can be used. Unlike traditional music therapy, psychosonics places little importance on the performance aspect of music. As many musicians know, practicing and performing occupy the mind in a way that allows escape from self-awareness rather than exploration. While success at task-oriented activities may play a part in positive reinforcement of a person's self-image, in music the risk of failing remains high because of the complexity of skill involved. There are more persons who have tried to perform and given up than who have succeeded.

Basic Principles

From my experience in teaching the class on Mahler, I realized certain things that have become basic to psychosonics. The first has to do with the body's sensory receptors. The mind is most attentive to the sensory information received by the eye, so that in listening with one's eyes open there is a large amount of mental processing taking place on the visual plane. Closing one's eyes allows for greater awareness of hearing, as well as feeling. Another basic principle has to do with body posture. Everyone I have worked with has reported increased listening and feeling attention when lying on his or her back or when moving in dancelike activities. A third important point deals with the source of sound. After considerable experience in various situations I am convinced that working in a live acoustic chamber increases the productivity enormously. A cavernous room with a high ceiling, such as found in a church or school, is best. In listening to recorded music, only a well-separated stereo system should be used, and of the highest fidelity one can afford. Finally, it is to be remembered that psychologically the music must be considered an extension of one's self. If the human animal were incapable of making any sounds within its own body, I doubt that any sounds heard from without would be capable of arousing self-expressive or self-meaningful content. The fact that we can make sounds within our bodies is the source of projections that give meanings to the sounds we hear, and certainly to those we create with our inventions and instruments. While some of these points may seem simplistic, their being overlooked has resulted in considerably less success.

Self-Generated Sound

The first major area of therapeutic endeavor is discovery of the body's own sounds. The exercises are not designed to "train" a person in singing or any other predetermined concept of "correct" sound. They are planned to help people be in touch with their own sounds. That is not always easily accomplished, since many will resist all of their own possibilities while trying to construct mental concepts of what they think they should sound like and then producing sounds to match those fabricated concepts.

In this area of work a trained therapist in psychosonics can tell by the sounds—the overtones, resonance, and sources—how in touch a person is with his or her own body. The body and feelings are a holistic unit, and in self-generated sound exercises the work is with the body.

The half-dozen exercises discussed below deal with specific aspects of therapy related to breathing, physical tension, and sexual energy. They are designed to help people be in touch with the reality of the animal body. When practiced daily over a period of six months they have contributed to creating energy in cases of depression, helped persons to feel centered and present, aided in the release of physical inhibition, and in certain types of psychosomatic illness contributed to healing.

Attention and Concentration

Before attempting to use music in listening therapy, some preparation in developing attention is usually necessary. For some, this training may take up to twelve weeks. The work consists of listening to specially prepared "concentration forms" and "path patterns." The process in itself has therapeutic benefit. In developing attention to the separate elements of music, the concentration required permits periods in which self-consciousness can be put aside. Furthermore, it enlarges the experience of body reality begun with self-generated sound by adding the awareness of time, space, and sensing. Separate forms and patterns in (1) rhythm, (2) tempo, and (3) musical form create an awareness of time; (4) melody, (5) harmony, and (6) polyphony, an awareness of space; (7) tone color and (8) dynamics, a sensing in sound. These eight elements are the ingredients blended together in the experience we call music.

In one "concentration form" exercise the person sits or lies in front of stereo speakers and listens to a prerecorded synthesized tone. The tone lasts for approximately twelve to twenty-five minutes, during which time subtle changes take place in its overtone structure and tonal makeup. When the exercise is successful, it brings about an increase in attention, awareness, physical sensation, and feelings. Also, the person often feels relaxed and calm after the exercise.

Other synthesized tapes present sounds that subtly change motion, blend, and color. In one exercise, rhythmic patterns evolve with slow but continuous change, and in another there are two simultaneous melodic lines slowly changing in pitch. One taped exercise emphasizing color and dynamics encourages the participants to physically express in posture, facial expression, and motion the way the sounds feel to their senses.

When body contact is appropriate a recording with simultaneous evolving multiple rhythmic levels is played. One person lies down with eyes closed; others sit around the person, touching his or her arms, legs, head, and abdomen. While listening carefully to the music, each person finds one rhythmic level to communicate to the person lying down through pulsing touch and slow movement of the limbs. The person receiving the body contact allows his or her awareness to expand to hearing all the rhythmic levels.

The next step is to work with music itself. In the exercises bodily movement is utilized continually. Lines of sound are traced in space, rhythms are massaged on bodies, postures are assumed to represent sounds, and combinations of these movements take on dancelike characteristic. All this contributes to a growing sense of being and an awareness of present reality, limited in content as it is. I believe this sense of *I-am*–ness is essential in order for any self-growth to occur. Its presence seems necessary in psychological healing and may in itself be the catharsis that initiates the healing process. For one thing, it relieves the neurotic inner dialogue that separates us from reality. That helps to change the abstraction of oneself (thinking) into the reality of oneself (feeling).

Becoming Sound

It is the sense of *I am* that becomes the key to using music in a therapeutic way. Much of our experience with music is based on a subject-object relationship: that we are listeners to something outside ourselves upon which we make judgments (I like—I don't like) and raise questions (What is it?—How is it?). The purpose of psychosonics is to replace this objective thinking of judgments and questions about the other with a subjective projection that says, "I am this music—this music is me." This mental attitude replaces object-listening with body-listening.

Movement

The most obvious level in which that can take place is movement in its broadest sense, or dance. In the movement exercise we actually attempt to become the sound. The music may or may not be considered danceable, the point being that attention is not on dancing or creating a dance but on being sound incarnate. How well we hear will be clearly visible in our bodily movements. It is at this point that the therapist must act as a dispensing agent in prescribing the appropriate music for creating the right experience for the individual's next step in growth. A therapist with a broad musical background and a good sense of human intuition will create an experience in movement that will put people in touch with some aspect of their being worth working on. After the exercise in becoming the sound through movement, the verbal process begins. For the first time we begin to employ memory and words by "retelling the tale" of our experience.

Fantasy

More specific structuring of this use of music can involve fantasy and psychodrama. Selecting music for fantasy work requires a large knowledge of repertory. The fantasy may be guided, in which the therapist describes part of the scene; or free, where no suggestions are provided. Again, the "retelling the tale" becomes the occasion for further work in verbal encounter or Gestalt.

Using music in psychodrama is like providing the soundtrack to a film. In psychosonics the emphasis is on allowing the music to suggest the scene being played, rather than vice versa, with only occasional help from the therapist acting as director.

In the experiences using music in movement and fantasy a person comes in touch with material from the unconscious and memory. The material can be dealt with in verbal therapy in the same manner as is usual for dreams, fantasies, and memories.

In one such fantasy experiment, music based on the myth of Sisyphus is played while the participants are "directed" in role-playing the scenes being depicted. Participants exert physical strength pushing fantasied boulders up mountains only to remain standing at the top watching their efforts fail as the stone rolls down and the whole process is begun again. After the experience, the group talks about what they felt and what associative content may have surfaced. Specific salient points are then followed up with individual Gestalt techniques. In most cases the music session provides the material for the important verbal work, whereas in the self-generated sound and movement exercises the therapeutic experience is a direct nonverbal one.

Adjunctive Therapy

In most of the procedures that I have described for using music or sound, it is assumed that some form of psychological awareness is present in the therapist. A strictly musical experience may have no psychological benefit beyond recreation and relaxation. However, when music is used as an adjunctive therapy real work is taking place within the person. The work may not have the qualities of recreation, but instead may contain frustration, discipline, and some emotional pain. It should also eventually contain feelings of joy, freedom, and the desire to continue growing.

This therapy does not originate as primarily a treatment for psychotic disorders, but exists for the psycho-social neuroses that prevent self-actualization at various levels of life. These may be the fears of individuality and creativity of the adolescent; the ennui, paranoia, anxiety, and depression of a vast number of our adult population; the hopeless and lonely existence of the aged.

The goal is to bring back humanizing and spiritual dimensions to existence. Music is potentially one more technique by which that can be accomplished. It is an entirely new approach to music from that of the development of Western culture, with its emphasis on aesthetic design and public entertainment. With the contribution of recorded music all the world's musical expressions are available to us for highly personal and private use. A young generation listening to music through stereo headphones while lying on water beds discovered things not possible in churches and concert halls. A decade of growing numbers of meditators has brought new awareness to understanding the oneness of music and listener.

The most significant trend in the realization that music is no longer regarded merely as a subject-object relationship is in musical composition itself. There are a few composers today who create music with no other intention than to affect the psyche of the listener. According to the old ways of listening this music might be quite boring. But in terms of experiencing one's self, or sensory awareness, or meditative states, this music is entirely effective. As one of my students who is writing such music said, "My music is not designed to call attention to itself, but to draw the listener's attention into greater self-awareness and communication with the spaces of his or her own mind and being."

Janet Chase-Marshall

———•———

Poems Struggling to Be Born

Poetry has slipped from the place of eminence it once held in Western society when verse was widely believed to be the highest form of human expression and poets such as Lord Byron were great culture heroes, with the kind of status we reserve today for film stars and athletes. Yet poetry continues to move deeply through the lives of many people, and in its new incarnation as a mode of therapy—reported here by a contributing editor to Human Behavior *magazine—it appears to be alive and well and useful.*

"Every poet," said T. S. Eliot in the '30s, "would like to be able to think he had some direct utility. As things are, poetry is not a career."

Had Eliot, poet and visionary, been born a few years later, he might have found a place in a brand-new professional calling —poet as therapist (or therapist as poet).

Actually, the curative powers of poetry have been suspected for quite a while: Aristotle could not recommend highly enough emotional catharsis through verse and drama. The poet Sophocles discovered and chronicled the Oedipus complex about 2100 B.F. (Before Freud). And the god Apollo handily ruled over the twin arts of poetry and medicine. Freud himself claimed that poets salvaged "from the whirlpool of their emotions the deepest truths to which we others have to force our way, ceaselessly groping among tortuous uncertainties."

Source: This essay originally appeared in *Human Behavior*, August 1973, pp. 24–28. Copyright © 1973 *Human Behavior* Magazine. Reprinted by permission.

In 1973, there are at least 400 therapists using poetry to treat at least 3,500 drug addicts and alcoholics, mental retardates and schizophrenics, children, adolescents, and the elderly and those who will always look for new ways to self-actualize.

There is a Poetry Therapy Institute on the West Coast and an Association for Poetry Therapy on the East, and in between there are sundry poets, librarians, psychologists, doctors, and social workers practicing and teaching the old-new discipline.

Success stories for the new "therapeutic triumph" are already legend among practitioners and touts. There are the seven hard-core schizophrenics who had been unsuccessfully treated for an average of six years in Dixmont State Hospital in Pittsburgh with medication, electric shock and traditional individual and group therapies. But after eight months of once-a-week poetry therapy sessions, three were discharged and the other four were making regular home visits. There are the narcotics addicts who, as one therapist puts it, go from mainlining heroin to maintaining on methadone to getting high on poetry. There is Francisco, the tough young New York street gang member who was completely reformed after exposure to the wonder of Homer's *Iliad*. Apparently, there is no task too large for the word of a poet, or as certain poetry therapists would have it—"a rhyme for all reasons!"

The first formal poetry therapy program was initiated in 1959 by psychiatrist Jack Leedy and the late poet Eli Greifer at Brooklyn's Cumberland Hospital. Ten years later, Leedy founded the Association for Poetry Therapy, which this April hosted the first World Poetry Therapy Conference in New York.

In 1971, Arthur Lerner, holder of psychology and English doctorates, founded the Poetry Therapy Institute in Los Angeles quite separate of parallel movements begun in the East. Lerner claims the title of "first poetry therapist and poet-in-residence at a private mental health facility"—i.e., Woodview-Calabasas Neuropsychiatric Center in the San Fernando Valley. (Leedy had already taken that title for a public institution.) Although both men seemingly seek to spread the self-same poetic word, Lerner has refused to jump on anyone else's bandwagon and is accordingly loudly piloting his own.

But ideological differences aside, they all would agree that the poem is an agent of communication—sort of an intermediary or extra facilitator beween therapist and client. It's an adjunctive tool that mixes well with almost any psychological school or personality theory. Many people, it's said, can more easily say things from behind verse, their own or someone else's, that may be too painful to say straight out. While a single reading of Whitman or Dickinson may not cure, Lerner admits, it can "loosen large chunks of rigidity and help facilitate verbal and nonverbal communication.

"Instead of rationalizing, projecting, compensating, or identifying, we can deal with the poem as another person in a non-threatening manner," he continues. Echoes Leedy, "Poetry is an 'understanding someone.' "

Psychologist Charles Crootof, a contributor to the Leedy-edited book simply titled *Poetry Therapy*, published in 1969, says that because the poet shares himself, it's easier for the patient to express his own feelings in response. "The poet's feelings function as a resonator in the patient's psyche, where corresponding fragments of memory and experience start to vibrate sympathetically, are shaken loose from their submerged mooring, and rise to the surface, where they can be looked at in the daylight of reality."

While poetry therapists generally agree on what a poem is supposed to do, they differ on how to do it. Some urge patients on with inspirational poetry while others use verse in confrontive or Gestalt styles, or to stimulate free association or as an unblocking device. Some emphasize reading poetry in contrapuntal fashion (a poem to answer a poem); others encourage patients to express themselves with original work.

Jack Leedy invokes the isoprinciple, which he borrowed from music therapy: to be therapeutic, a poem should ideally express the mood or emotional state of the patient. He also encourages poetry written in round-robin fashion—each patient contributing one line to build poetic moods. The late Smiley Blanton, a New York psychiatrist, went even further to match poem to mood, prescribing specific poems for bereavement, depression, decision making, nervous tension, fear of responsibility and unrequited love. Thus, as a nerve tonic, patients read Swinburne's "Love at Sea";

> We are in love's land to-day;
> Where shall we go?
> Love, shall we start or stay,
> Or sail or row?
> There's many a wind and way,
> And never a May but May;
> We are in love's land to-day;
> Where shall we go?

And for love's labours lost, something from Browning:

> You'll love me yet! and I can tarry
> Your love's protracted growing:
> . . . You'll look at least on love's remains,
> A grave's one violet:
> Your look?—that pays a thousand pains.
> What's death? You'll love me yet.

Arthur Lerner's therapeutic sessions are punctuated by a continual flitting from poem to poem, never pausing for very long to rest on any one poem, one person, one problem.

"Does anyone have a poem they want to read?" Lerner or an aide will ask to kick off a session.

After the initial offering is made, Lerner is then likely to immediately ask again, "Would someone like to answer that with another poem?" But poems offered as a response can sometimes be painfully mismatched, and some group members are too eager to get on to "sharing" their own work to search for someone else's answer.

One such group at California State University at Long Beach, co-led by Lerner trainee Don Weinstock, an English professor, and psychologist Carolyn Owen, places emphasis on writing. The group is a mecca for would-be poets. One intense, black-eyed poet read:

> OK, feelings, make way for solid matter!
> Make way for doin' it now!
> Make way for screams and grunts
> And tables and chairs and clouds of putrid smoke
> And bouncing words and pigs and even unseen events
> on the verge of pricking your damn tentacles. . . .

Exhausted, he looked around the room for reaction.

"What are you trying to say?" one small girl finally asked.

"That's just how I'm feeling, man," he explained.

"Does anyone else have a poem they'd like to read?" facilitated the facilitator.

Psychologists Kenneth Edgar and Richard Hazley are skeptical of this approach. "In forming a poetry therapy group, the psychologist might be wise to exclude that type of individual with literary ambitions cathected to the ideal image," they said. "Poetry therapy, in this case, would possibly increase the protagonist's arrogance and magnify the discrepancies between the actual and idealized self."

San Diego psychologist Joanna Lessner, who combines Gestalt and psychodrama with poetry, disagrees emphatically with the read-a-poem-a-minute approach. "It's simply too much input to continuously read one poem after another," she said. "Expression for its own sake is not enough."

Lessner will read a particular poem ("it's always open-ended, not closed or inspirational or leading to easy answers") to evoke reaction. Then group members assume and experience a single aspect. This way, she says, "the participant may dramatically face himself and learn to see and feel new ways of being."

A poem she has found to evoke very different responses is Lawrence Ferlinghetti's "Poem #8" from *A Coney Island of the Mind*:

In Golden Gate Park that day
                    a man and his wife were coming along
            thru the enormous meadow
                        which was the meadow of the world
He was wearing green suspenders
                    and carrying an old beat-up flute
                                in one hand
        while his wife had a bunch of grapes
                    which she kept handing out
                                individually
                to various squirrels
                            as if each
                    were a little joke

And then the two of them came on
                              thru the enormous meadow
which was the meadow of the world
                                   and then
           at a very still spot where the trees dreamed
         and seemed to have been waiting thru all time
                                              for them
            they sat down together on the grass
                          without looking at each other
                and ate oranges
                          without looking at each other
                               and put the peels
         in a basket which they seemed
                          to have brought for that purpose
                without looking at each other
and then
              he took his shirt and undershirt off
           but kept his hat on
                              sideways
                              and without saying anything
           fell asleep under it
                         And his wife just sat there looking
    at the birds which flew about
      calling to each other
                         in the stilly air
           as if they were questioning existence
                         or trying to recall something forgotten

But then finally
              she too lay down flat
                         and just lay there looking up
                                   at nothing
                 yet fingering the old flute
                                   which nobody played
               and finally looking over
                              at him
           without any particular expression
                              except a certain awful look
                 of terrible depression

In Lessner's groups, members have chosen to be flutes ("I don't like just being carried around and held. I want to be played"); and grass ("I want so much to push out of the soil and grow, but it's pretty hard sometimes"); and orange peels ("They toss me away when I'm no longer useful").

A 17-year-old girl wrote her own poem about her identification with the grapes:

> I am the grapes
> entering the hands of others
> to be devoured.
> Each section to be taken off alone
> not connected with any other part
> of the plant—
> Continually giving to reaching arms,
> Always feeling the last grape is
> to be picked off the vine.
> Somehow more grapes keep
> growing.
> As long as I am a grape
> I hope always to keep growing.
> But somewhere along the line,
> I'd like a raisin in return.

Lessner doesn't push her clients to write poetry. "Some people don't write poetry to make contact, but really to blow wind," she said. "To me, this is totally destructive and time wasting—just a vocal neurotic verbalization that doesn't accomplish anything.

"In one of my groups, I had a middle-aged, barely literate and not particularly culturally endowed woman who was going through a hellish divorce," she elaborated. "Another woman— a sort of pseudointellectual—wrote a poem to the first woman's loneliness, but she just couldn't understand it."

There is disagreement about the value of original work. Lerner says, "It is vital to attain a state of sound personality integration, adding a dimension of personal meaning to the creator's life." And Yale psychiatrist Albert Rothenberg states, "Learning to write good poetry in the course of therapy can also help a patient to gain a sense of mastery. In fact, poetry is even more revelatory than dreams."

But can anyone, even the neighborhood dullard, respond to poetry therapy? Yes, choruses every one of its practitioners wth evangelical enthusiasm. "People who are barely literate love it," says Lerner. "Remember, we're talking about the heart."

"It's worth trying in all types of cases," Leedy adds. "A lot of people may say they hate poetry, but as they get into it with simple poetry, they start to like it."

Jo Lessner has a minor reservation. "Since poetry is directed to such heterogeneous groups, and heard rather than seen, the language must be easily and universally understandable," she cautions. If it's got archaic or florid language, overly complex syntax, and highly structured verse, Lessner says it's going to be ineffective. "The more open the form, the greater the freedom of response."

For that reason, another poem she has found extremely valuable is Langston Hughes's "Dream Deferred":

> What happens to a dream deferred:
> Does it dry up
> like a raisin in the sun?
> Or fester like a sore—
> And then run?
> Does it stink like rotten meat?
> Or crust and sugar over—
> like a syrupy sweet?
> Maybe it just sags
> like a heavy load.
> Or does it explode?

Poetry has been especially effective with drug addicts, according to Leedy. "The way I see it, let's turn drug addicts into poetry addicts," he booms enthusiastically. "You know, from heroin to Homer to Herrick. After all, no one has died from an overdose of poetry."

Ruth Lisa Schecter, poetry therapist at one of New York's drug treatment centers, Odyssey House, said, "For residents, poetry therapy is a constructive tool for ventilating unspeakable problems."

After sitting silently at several group meetings, a young black resident of Odyssey House wrote her first poem:

> when i was running
> what was i running from?
> are there any questions?
> are there any answers?
> was it my mother?
> give me some answers . . . please
> i was never running alone
> relatives, friends, family too
> yeah, family too ain't it a shame?
> . . . but four months ago i stopped running
> 'cause i'm not afraid anymore.

"The nice thing about introducing poetry to addicts," said psychiatrist Rothenberg, "is that it's a very straight statement. You're telling them there's something valuable in your world, something they might get some advantage from."

Since 1968, Dr. Bill Barkley has used poetry therapy with inmates of the California Men's Colony Medical Facility in San Luis Obispo, California. Though many of his clients are serving sentences for murder and sexual offenses, Barkley claims the convicts' poetry is neither morbid nor vulgar, but revolves around themes of love, fear and rejection. "It is surprisingly beautiful," he says.

Poetry also seems to be successful with children. "It's really beautiful there," says Lerner. "You don't have to explain; they pick it up, and you can make stories and games and free-associate all over the place." It's also been used with the deaf ("it brings out a great deal of their inner language").

For schizophrenics, poetry is a "language closer to them than the language of mothers, newspapers or doctors," says a psychiatrist who uses it in a private mental hospital. In fact, "the language of the schizophrenic is extremely poetic," suggests Jo Lessner. "They are symbolic, use lots of neologisms and put things in order with a startling inner logic—not bound by grammatical and other inhibitions."

Emily Dickinson and her themes of ironic loneliness hold great appeal for adolescents:

> I'm Nobody! Who are you?
> Are you—Nobody—too?
> Then there's a pair of us!
> Don't tell!
> (They'd banish us—you know!)

But poetry doesn't necessarily speak to every adolescent. Lerner aide Leon Love, a burly, black ex-professional football player, counsels a group of young Chicanos and blacks with poetry at Jackson High School in central Los Angeles. Many of them have police records; all were sent to Jackson because they had been failing or had been expelled from other schools.

Usually uncontrollably vociferous, they remained impassively silent at one session while Love and others zapped verse after verse at them. Later asked if he liked or understood poetry, one boy just shook his head quickly from side to side. Yet Love says they have become more responsive since starting poetry therapy. "A few of these guys write poetry now," he says, "and they all dig it when I give them books to take home."

To its ardent adherents, there is little poetry therapy cannot do. "I like to think," says Jack Leedy, "that many illnesses—ulcers, colitis, migraine, and fatigue—are really poems struggling to be born."

Poetry therapy potentially allows large numbers of people untrained in specific psychotherapeutic techniques to enter the mental health field. Ideally, says Leedy, a group should be headed by a psychiatrist well-versed in literature and a psychologically oriented poet. Arthur Lerner, who teaches poetry therapy at UCLA and Los Angeles City College, says, "My facilitators can work alone or under supervision, but they know their limitations."

Of course, not everybody loves poetry therapy. It has been likened, by it detractors, to "a nice warm back rub" and "another therapy gimmick added to a hundred other relatively useless tools we already possess."

It is possible, Rothenberg warns the incautious, to "only learn to hide feelings with poetry and never direct them toward the people or situations where they apply. One of the roots of mental illness is just such an inability to express feelings or deal with conflicts directly."

The artistic results of poetry produced in therapy range from the sublime to the sassy to the silent. Pulitzer Prize–winning poet Anne Sexton first wrote poetry when she was in a mental hospital.

> I speed through the antiseptic tunnel
> where the moving dead
> still talk of pushing their bones
> against the thrust of cure.

A rather droll patient penned a special poem for his therapist:

> Cough up, you bastard
> Make with the poems or
> Your leader will give you
> a friendly, accepting, not too happy look,
> a sidelong sigh, an embarrassing look,
> a message quite simple that says without doubt:
> you tried, but then after all you're a schnook.

Psychiatrist Sidney Sharman, a poetry therapist from Rye, England, tells of how "I killed a poet." An unhappy poet came to Sharman asking for help. Sharman induced him to write poetry to purge his own demons. When Sharman pronounced his patient cured, the once-muse gave up the word and became a successful businessman. The world may have lost a neurotic poet, but it gained another success.

Thomas C. Greening

---•---

The Uses of Autobiography

Therapy and autobiography have always been closely related: psycho-analysis is one kind of autobiographical structure, journal keeping is another, and counseling practices of all persuasions include the re-counting of personal experiences and the search for meanings and patterns in them. Even modes of therapy most resolutely committed to the "here and now" recognize that the unfinished business of the past keeps turning up in the present, that the individual today is part of the complex gestalt of a total human life. Thomas Greening, therapist and editor of the Journal of Humanistic Psychology, *surveys the art of autobiography from a psychologist's viewpoint and considers some of its uses for the reader and the writer.*

Introduction

As a psychotherapist, I spend much of my life listening to the stories of people's lives, searching with them to find meaning in their pasts, experience the present, fill in mysterious gaps, re-construct their identities, and build more satisfying futures. I am continually engaged in drawing out the autobiographies of others, and as I do this I use and expand my own autobiograph-ical consciousness. I am helped in my work by my awareness of my own history as a sometimes useful first approximation to the experience of others, and my professional training and per-

SOURCE: This essay is a revision of a lecture originally presented at the Reed College Humanities Research Center, March 11, 1969. Copy-right © 1977 by Thomas C. Greening. Printed by permission of the author.

sonal psychoanalysis have supposedly helped me to be alert to the possible distortions I tend to introduce into my perceptions of others owing to the idiosyncrasies of my own life history.

What I say here will be limited to the perspective of a clinical psychologist who has reviewed his own life history at some length, listened to the life histories of hundreds of people, and read a few autobiographies, but who has no claim to being a literary critic or student of the history of autobiography. My hope is that I may contribute something toward a cross-fertilization in which psychology may add to our understanding of autobiography and autobiography may become more centrally utilized in the creation of a relevant psychology of human experience.

My Early Encounters with Autobiography

I grew up in a small town, was an only child, and, owing to my own timidity and a somewhat sheltered environment, remained rather naïve about the wide world of action and the deep world of experiencing. Books were one way out: "out" in the sense of escape, and "out" in the sense of growth. I will mention a few of the books I read, to illustrate the way in which the lives of real people we read about become entwined with our own. My father recommended I read *Two Years before the Mast* by Richard Henry Dana and I did so. The fact that he recommended it was significant. We were not a highly literate family in which books were commonly recommended to me. Thus I concluded that there must indeed be something special about this book. Furthermore, his way of recommending it suggested that it was not some sort of moral duty but rather a possibly enjoyable story. When I was younger he had read aloud to me one story of sea and adventure, *Treasure Island,* and now here was another story, a true one, about a young man who goes into the world. What a surprise to find that Dana was a rather frustrated fellow from a proper Boston home who shipped out because he was not able to settle down as a "well-adjusted" Harvard student. Was I to believe that others really had that kind of difficulty, that they took such drastic steps to find themselves, and that my father thought such a story safe or desirable reading for me? Well, Dana sailed to California and loaded hides from what is now called Dana Point, and when I am down by that part of the coast I meditate a little on the elaborate combination of forces that brought me, many years later, to the same restlessness and the same part of the globe.

Maybe what I've sought most of all in autobiography are fathers and brothers. We need all the help we can get in forming our identities, and one father is never enough. Two whom I found in my confused college years were Sigmund Freud and Arthur Koestler, and the autobiographical elements in their writings were essential for my identification with them. As I prepared this paper I very movingly reexperienced a crucial phase of my late adolescence when Freud and Koestler guided me into whole realms of new territory, tearing down miles of barricades in my mind.

Here was Freud, dignified Victorian family man and scientist, speaking to me with sober but intense perceptiveness about sex and emotions. He took my struggles seriously, devoted a majestic career to such concerns, and built a whole scientific theory around the kind of personality development I was awkwardly grappling with. He described his own dreams and experiences and revealed himself as a creature not entirely unlike me, in spite of his infinitely greater capacity to transcend his conflicts and use them creatively. He was an identification model showing me that intelligence is a vital force that can conquer fear, guilt, and despair. He was saying that people are important, that we don't know enough about ourselves, and that a fantastic amount goes on inside us. You may take that for granted, but no one had ever got that message across to me as bluntly as Freud did. I had grown up following a Sunday school version of Christianity, admiring Thomas Edison and Henry Ford, and believing that a man's task was to apply math, physics, and mechanics to create the good life. Freud was my first guide to the inner person.

Koestler was my first guide to political awareness. His autobiographical chapter in *The God That Failed* and his autobiography, *Arrow in the Blue*, helped me experience through the senses of a living man the social and historical events and issues I had studied intellectually and abstractly through news-

papers and college classes.[1] I read *Darkness at Noon* and won-
dered if I and contemporary history would ever meet in such
close quarters as Rubashov and Ivanov, or as Koestler and his
potential executioners in Spain.[2] While I was wondering that,
I met Koestler himself. He spent a week at my college, and for
that time I did not have to settle for dim glimpses of the writer
behind the novel or the autobiographical ex-Communist in a
book: I could talk with him directly in seminars and conversa-
tions, gratifying my undergraduate craving to learn about life
and borrow an identity.

Freud and Koestler grew up in Vienna. My arrival in Vienna
a year later to study was not consciously based on the fact that
it was their home. But there I was, eight blocks from Berggasse,
where Freud lived for forty-seven years, walking the streets where
Koestler first saw twentieth-century history beginning to march.

It meant a great deal to me in those days that there were such
men who expressed a deep caring for human welfare, combined
that with sophisticated intellectual analysis, and devised powerful plans of action for pushing at the course of history. I realized
I had to find my own way, and that grandiose identifications with
heroes could be dangerous, but it helped to feel some bond,
however symbolic and contrived, with men who had confronted
similar issues.

How Autobiography Affects Readers

I have tried to convey that my reading of autobiography was
truly a formative influence on my personal development. The
process by which the reading of printed words affects the inner
nature and subsequent behavior of a reader is, however, very
difficult to describe. I'd like to know more about what concrete
results are produced by reading autobiography and how they
come about. I have referred to the way in which autobiography
may meet a need for identification models, expanded conceptions

1. Richard Crossman, ed., *The God That Failed* (New York: Harper &
Brothers, 1950) ; Arthur Koestler, *Arrow in the Blue* (New York: Macmillan,
1952) .
2. Arthur Koestler, *Darkness at Noon* (New York: Macmillan, 1941) .

of life, alternative pathways for development, and reduction of one's sense of alienation and strangeness. I believe we never simply read an autobiography; we read it and concurrently review our own life and plan our future.

Simon Lesser in his book *Fiction and the Unconscious* describes many of the needs we seek to gratify by reading, and most of his analysis is equally relevant to autobiography.[3] He refers to our need for pleasurable fantasy relief from the frustrating finiteness of our real lives; our need to work through the anger, depression, and guilt produced by harboring impulses that clash with civilization; and our wish to be awakened and "turned on" to feelings and possibilities nascent within us.

Lesser's chapter "The Processes of Response" is one of the best discussions I have read of the ways in which literature meets these needs. Briefly, the four key principles are aesthetic ambiguity, psychic distance, nonverbal evocation, and analogizing.

Aesthetic Ambiguity

The story we read, fictional or autobiographical, must be concrete, specific, and vivid enough for us to see and believe it, but it must also generate a surplus of responses, a rich complexity of nonspecific associations, an ambiguous reverberation within us. Even when presented with the detail and factual accuracy of a compulsive autobiography, we must have room for our own imaginations to enter into the creative process whereby the author's life becomes "real" for us.

Psychic Distance

The precise amount of psychic distance and closeness we need in order to feel emotionally involved and yet able to endure the suspense, pain, and even joy will vary greatly depending on our own capacity to tolerate intense experience and the author's ambitions regarding how hard he wants to hit us. Images, language, and dramatic structure all may be regulated by the author

---

3. Simon Lesser, *Fiction and the Unconscious* (Boston: Beacon Press, 1957).

in attempting to control the degree and type of reader response. But especially in the case of autobiography, other factors within the reader and largely outside the control of the writer, such as preexisting identification with the protagonist, will influence the psychic distance and thus the intensity of the reader's experience.

Nonverbal Evocation

Nonverbal evocation is of special interest to me as a psychotherapist. Psychotherapy as I practice it is primarily a verbal process. How can I select words, and help my patients find words, that will penetrate the defenses of intellectualization, isolation of effect, and plain old repression to reach buried feeling? Lesser describes how the formal structure and the language of fiction are selected to reach the reader at many levels:

> The concrete, sensory language of fiction single-handedly fosters the kind of anxiety-free perception toward which form strives; *it quickly and effectively transmits almost any kind of material without requiring the reader to put what he understands into words.* Though composed of words, so far as its reception is concerned the language of fiction is an instrument of non-discursive communication.
>
> . . . for the most part the images register upon our minds *as images.* Only occasionally is their meaning—or, at any rate, a considerable portion of their meaning—transcribed into words. There is no need for such transcriptions. Untranscribed, the images are not only understandable, but possessed of more vividness and immediacy than is usually attached to words.
>
> . . . we formulate no more than a small portion of what we understand when we read fiction, and we are particularly unlikely to formulate perceptions which would arouse anxiety if made explicit. Obviously a language which lends itself to this kind of partial and selective apprehension is an ideal one for dealing with emotional problems. It encourages honesty without jeopardizing security; it permits things to be said and understood without being conceptualized and brought to awareness.[4]

I would not place as much stress as Lesser on the value of avoiding anxiety and conceptualization altogether, but I agree

4. *Ibid.,* pp. 153, 154.

with his basic point. The task is to evoke feeling and aid the
ego in authentic integrations of experience, without producing
disruptive anxiety, repressive superego action, or dry, staid ego
formulations.

Let us pursue an example here. Both Freud and D. H. Lawrence
were strongly attached to their mothers, and their lives and writings bear a deep imprint from their very special mother-son
relationships. Both men presented to their readers the distillation
of their experience but used different forms and techniques to
do so. Freud developed his theory of the Oedipus complex as a
central developmental struggle for boys, while Lawrence gave us
an unforgettable story of his own struggle in his autobiographical
novel, *Sons and Lovers*. Freud published one of his basic papers
on the subject in 1912, and Lawrence's novel was published in
1913. Lesser compares the two approaches to the subject as
follows:

> From Lawrence's novel the dissecting intelligence of the critic can
> abstract the main ideas Freud develops in his paper; and it is
> worthwhile to abstract them—doing so may help the critic to
> crystallize certain of his impressions of the book. But whereas
> Freud labored to bring his ideas before us as clearly as possible, it
> would not be an exaggeration to say that Lawrence was determined
> that we should *not* have "ideas," that we should not think con-
> ceptually, as we read his story. More accurately, he had a different
> objective: to engage us emotionally, to induce us to share the
> experiences of his characters; and he intuitively recognized that he
> could not achieve this objective if he spoke to the intellect alone.
> Lawrence himself, as Aldous Huxley has pointed out, "refused to
> know abstractly." As man and as artist, he felt driven to render his
> story with as much concreteness, vividness and immediacy as he
> could muster. The scenes and incidents must speak for themselves,
> and they speak in a language which is vaguer but richer and
> more stirring than the language of intellectual discourse.[5]

Unfortunately, Freud was devoted to abstract intellectual
discourse at the expense of evocative writing, even though his
courageous step of writing about his own dreams and his vivid
narratives in his letters tantalize us with the possibility of what

5. *Ibid.*, p. 177.

an exciting document his autobiography could have been. The brief autobiography we have from him is, regrettably and ironically, mainly an essay rather than the felt experience of a man's life. Lawrence's fictionalized autobiography tells us more about Lawrence than Freud's conventional autobiography tells us about Freud.

Analogizing

The analogizing function of the reader is perhaps the most important of all, especially if we read autobiography with the explicit intention of gaining something to use in our own lives. Lesser uses the term "analogizing" to refer to that process by which we create a parallel, interwoven story about ourselves as we read about a fictional or autobiographical character. We unconsciously join in the events, try ourselves out vicariously, and branch off from the story line with our private version of similar scenes. We identify with many of the characters and take advantage of the aesthetic ambiguity of the work to evolve relevance and richness tailored to our own dynamics. This analogizing proceeds in a rapid, largely unconscious manner, so that we avoid being stalled or panicked by too blatant an intrusion of our own conflicts.

Autobiography has a certain advantage over fiction, at least initially, in stimulating analogizing in the reader. This is because we begin our reading of an autobiography with a receptive belief that the author really existed as a human being, and probably we have some preexisting tendency to identify with and admire him or her. Nevertheless, to make full use of this advantage, autobiography must use the basic devices of fiction to draw us into an experiential involvement. It was this analogizing process that I was attempting to illustrate earlier by describing my own involvement with the autobiographies and lives of Freud and Koestler.

One passage of Koestler's in particular stands out as an example of autobiographical writing with a high capacity to stimulate the analogizing process in me. This capacity results from the impactful nature of the event described, the effectiveness of the writing, and the striking parallel between Koestler's experience

and my own. This last factor, of course, is not under the control
of the writer, so that the degree to which an autobiography or
a particular passage stimulates analogizing is to a large degree
dependent upon fortuitous overlap between the writer's experience and the reader's. We may argue that a great writer could
stimulate analogizing in most readers, but it certainly helps if
the reader brings to his or her interaction with the autobiography
some relevant experiences of his or her own, be they conscious
or unconscious. Here is the passage by Koestler to which I responded:

> All my earliest memories seem to group themselves about three
> dominant themes: guilt, fear, and loneliness.
>   Of the three, fear stands out most vividly and persistently. My
> formative experiences seem to consist of a series of shocks.
>   The first that I remember occurred when I was between four and
> five years old. My mother dressed me with special care, and we went
> for an outing with my father. This in itself was unusual; but even
> more peculiar was the strange and apologetic manner of my parents
> as they led me down Andrassy Street, holding on firmly to both my
> hands. We were to visit Dr. Neubauer, they said; he was going to
> take a look at my throat and give me a cough medicine. After-
> wards, as a reward, I was to have some ice-cream.
>   I had already been taken to Dr. Neubauer the week before. He
> had examined me, and had then whispered with my parents in a
> manner which had aroused my apprehensions. This time we were
> not kept waiting; the doctor and his woman assistant were expect-
> ing us. Their manner was oily in a sinister way. I was made to sit
> in a kind of dentist's chair; then, without warning or explanation,
> my arms and legs were tied with leather straps to the frame of the
> chair. This was done with quick, deft movements by the doctor and
> his assistant, whose breathing was audible in the silence. Half
> senseless with fear, I craned my neck to look into my parents'
> faces, and when I saw that they, too, were frightened the bottom
> fell out of the world. The doctor hustled them both out of the
> room, fastened a metal tray beneath my chin, pried my chattering
> teeth apart, and forced a rubber gag beween my jaws.
>   There followed several indelible minutes of steel instruments
> being thrust into the back of my mouth, of choking and vomiting
> blood into the tray beneath my chin; then two more attacks with the
> steel instruments, and more choking and blood and vomit. That
> is how tonsillectomies were performed, without anaesthesia, A.D.

1910 in Budapest. I don't know how other children reacted to that kind of thing. In all probability I must have been sensitivised by some earlier, forgotten traumatic experience, for I reacted with a shock that was to have a lasting effect.

Those moments of utter loneliness, abandoned by my parents, in the clutches of a hostile and malign power, filled me with a kind of cosmic terror. It was as if I had fallen through a manhole, into a dark underground world of archaic brutality. Thenceforth I never lost my awareness of the existence of that second universe into which one might be transported, without warning, from one moment to the other. The world had become ambiguous, invested with a double meaning; events moved on two different planes at the same time—a visible and an invisible one—like a ship which carries its passengers on its sunny decks, while its keel ploughs through the dark phantom world beneath.

It is not unlikely that my subsequent preoccupation with physical violence, terror, and torture derives partly from this experience, and that Dr. Neubauer paved the way for my becoming a chronicler of the more repulsive aspects of our time. This was my first meeting with "Ahor"—the irrational, Archaic Horror—which subsequently played such an important part in the world around me that I designed this handy abbreviation for it. When, years later, I fell into the hands of the regime which I dreaded and detested most, and was led in handcuffs through a hostile crowd, I had the feeling that this was but a repetition of a situation I had already lived through—that of being tied, gagged, and delivered to a malign power. And when my friends perished in the clutches of Europe's various dictators, I could, in writing about them, without much effort put myself in their place.[6]

I read that passage with amazement and acute discomfort after I had already developed a strong identification with Koestler as a result of reading his books and meeting him. It seemed slightly uncanny to me to discover that as a child he had suffered a traumatic tonsillectomy with many details and consequences similar to my own. My strong response to reading this passage helped me become aware of the important formative effect of my tonsillectomy, with its feelings of abandonment, loneliness, terror, and physical pain. Mine was not as barbaric as Koestler's, nor did I later experience the analogous horrors of wartime

6. Koestler, *Arrow in the Blue*, pp. 32–33.

Europe. But subsequently, in psychoanalytic treatment, I came to realize the pervasive influence my tonsillectomy had on my way of experiencing life in general. I credit the reading of this passage of Koestler's with having started me on a process that eventually enabled me to get in touch with these deep-seated feelings.

Two years after reading Koestler's passage I happened to visit the small hospital where I had my tonsillectomy. Recalling how my reading of Koestler's passage had helped me work through some of my feelings, I paid a visit to the room where I had been confined so many years ago, and spent some time cheering up a small boy who occupied my former bed. I like to think of that as an example of how autobiographical writing can have a demonstrable impact on the reader's life and subsequently on the lives of others.

Autobiographies by Patients and Others

Autobiographies by patients and therapists have had particular significance to me in my development and have been increasingly significant in the field of psychotherapy.

An early classic by a patient was Clifford Beers's *A Mind That Found Itself*, written in 1907.[7] He wrote the book after having been hospitalized for a serious manic-depressive psychosis. His account has been widely reprinted and translated, and is credited by Gordon Allport with being "one of the most influential books in the entire history of psychology" and as having "led directly to the founding of the mental hygiene movement in America, and to the elimination of many of the institutional evils depicted in the story." That is high praise indeed, and if it is deserved it demonstrates how a seemingly narrow and pathological focus on one sick man can turn out to have widespread, health-enhancing consequences for the author and society.

I well remember my own experience in reading Beers's book; it was the first such book I had read about mental illness and

7. Clifford Beers, *A Mind That Found Itself* (Garden City, N.Y.: Double-day & Company, 1956) .

hospital care, and it influenced me to work as a psychiatric aide
one hot summer at Peoria State Hospital in Illinois. I'm not sure
I can say that the years that had elapsed since Beers published his
book have been time enough for the reforms he advocated to
be as clearly successful as Allport would have us believe. But
Beers did serve me well as a guide into some of the most for-
bidding territory a person can explore.

Benjamin Franklin, in contrast to Beers, is irritating to me
in his total omission of emotional conflicts and stressful developmental crises. Similarly, we only get glimpses of the so-called
"nervous illnesses" of Charles Darwin and Herbert Spencer, and
of Henry James's mysterious undiagnosed illness that kept him
out of the Civil War. Freud refers frequently to his neurasthenia
and dependence on cocaine in his letters, but in his autobiography we learn nothing of how he dealt with these problems
or how they were related, constructively or destructively, to the
rest of his life. Many such autobiographies seem to bear out the
accusation of Melvin Maddocks that "English autobiography is
a special art form whose genius is to combine an air of total
frankness with the practice of almost total discretion."

Three autobiographical writers who, although famous and
successful and not writing in the tradition of ex-patients, are
noteworthy for their painfully self-disclosing autobiographies—
Dag Hammarskjold, Eugène Ionesco, and Jean-Paul Sartre—all
present themselves as tormented men and give far more space
to the deficiency aspects of their lives than to the self-actualization
aspects, to use Maslow's terms.[8] Indeed, one could read all three
of their autobiographies or journals and not learn that the authors were highly creative and respected men in their fields.
Of course, Hammarskjold's and Ionesco's books are journals
rather than comprehensive autobiographies, so that might be
given as the reason for their focus on day-to-day inner struggles
rather than a broad perspective on development, achievement,
and satisfaction. But Hammarskjold believed that his edited
version of his journal was "the only true profile" of him. Sartre's

8. Dag Hammarskjold, *Markings*, trans. Leif Sjöberg and W. H. Auden
(New York: Alfred A Knopf, 1966) ; Eugène Ionesco, *Fragments of a Journal*,
trans. Jean Pace (New York: Grove Press, 1960) ; Jean-Paul Sartre, *Words*,
trans. Bernard Frechtman (New York: George Braziller, 1964) .

book is a true autobiography in scope, and it is equally concerned with the "case history" of himself. Few patients have written more anguished words about loneliness and "the frozen soul" behind the affable façade than Hammarskjold, or about the sense of deadness in the midst of life than Ionesco, or about the substitution of words and fantasies for authentic being than Sartre.

Perhaps a significant trend in recent autobiography is toward a less censored, less conventionally structured style of self-disclosure that includes honesty about defenses, games, and despair. If that is true, the distinction between sick and creative people becomes more blurred and useless than ever, and we may expect discussions of pathology in the autobiographies of successful people, and of courage and creativity in the autobiographies of patients.

Ionesco in particular represents this trend, since there are numerous indications that his journal was influenced by his own psychoanalytic treatment. Ironically, he even seems to place greater value on psychoanalytic self-exploration than on traditional attempts by writers, a somewhat unusual position for a literary man:

> Buber reminds us that, according to the Hasidim, the way begins with man's decisive exploration of his heart, but this exploration is only decisive if it really leads to the way, for there is a sort of investigation that is sterile, leading only to self-torture, despair and an even deeper entanglement. This reminds us of the purifying and exorcising function of psychoanalysis, contrasted with the self-analysis of men of letters and writers of journals which is futile and heart-rending.[9]

Unfortunately we are all aware that psychoanalysis is not always all that purifying and exorcizing, and there is some evidence that self-analysis by writers can be more than just futile and heart-rending. Ionesco serves as an enlightening example, however, of how the psychoanalytic patient and the writer may be merged and the resulting autobiographical writing may move through expressions of futility into psychoanalytic insight and emotional exorcism. At one point Ionesco wonders if his occa-

9. Ionesco, *Fragments of a Journal*, p. 58.

sional euphoria is due "to the fact that I am getting rid of my toxins by writing about them, that's to say projecting them outside myself."[10] His journal does have a quality of self-discovery and personal growth rather than mere repetitive analysis.

A paranoid German judge named Schreber wrote a bizarre book about his delusions and hospitalization.[11] He was convinced that civilization would benefit from knowledge of his experiences. Well, civilization did benefit, but only because Freud intervened as a psychoanalytic "translator" to make sense out of what would have otherwise been a forgotten chapter in the annals of insanity. Freud used the published version of Schreber's autobiography to document and develop his theory of paranoia and quotes from it extensively.[12] In gross contrast to the discreet and proper autobiographies of many public figures, Judge Schreber is embarrassingly self-disclosing about his blatantly perverse sexual fantasies. Efforts were made to prevent him from publishing his book, and the final version was highly censored. Nevertheless, we learn that Schreber believed that he had a mission to save the world and that to do this he must be transformed from a man into a woman and then have intercourse. His book is a classic example of a man's conscious intention to be honest and revealing but in that very attempt betraying to sophisticated readers his enormous ignorance of the unconscious and developmental sources of his ideas and fantasies. Freud explicates these sources in terms of Schreber's fixation on his father, sexual inhibition toward women, guilt over homosexual feelings, and withdrawal from investment in any acceptable, gratifying relationship. Schreber seemed oblivious to these sources, in spite of his leaving a trail of evidence that Freud could follow.

It is ironic and touching that although his fantasy of saving the world by becoming a woman sexually led him into unpro-

10. *Ibid.*, p. 78.
11. Daniel Paul Schreber, *Denkwürdigkeiten eines Nervenkranken* (Leipzig: Oswald, Mutzer, 1903; English ed.: *Memoirs of My Nervous Illness*, ed. and trans. Ida Macalpine and Richard A. Hunter [London: Dawson & Son, 1955]).
12. Sigmund Freud, "Psycho-Analytic Notes Upon an Autobiographical Account of a Case of Paranoia (Dementia Paranoides)," *Collected Papers*, trans. Alix Strachey and James Strachey (London: The Hogarth Press, 1953; New York: Basic Books, 1959), vol. 3, pp. 387–470.

ductive insanity, his writing of his story seemed to help him work through some of his problems and gave the world a valuable gift. He stated his intention thus: "I am of the opinion that it might be of advantage both to science and to the recognition of religious truths if, during my lifetime, qualified authorities were enabled to undertake some examination of my body and to hold some inquiry into my personal experiences. To this consideration all feelings of a personal character must yield."[13]

Freud took him at his word, and psychoanalytic theory is the richer for it.

In the history of psychological theory and treatment, another patient's autobiography stands as a landmark, and in this case we also have the benefit of commentary by a perceptive therapist, Marguerite Sechehaye. The story told by her patient Renée in *Autobiography of a Schizophrenic Girl* is one of the best accounts available of this illness and its treatment.[14] Sechehaye quotes Freud in her introduction: "These patients have turned away from outer reality; it is for this reason that they are more aware than we of inner reality and can reveal to us things which without them would remain impenetrable."[15]

Renée's autobiography is followed in the book by an "interpretation" section by her analyst, Sechehaye. This is a feature that might add to the significance of many autobiographies. It is rare that we have the opportunity to read a commentary by someone intimately involved in the autobiography we have just read. Many students of autobiography, such as Roy Pascal, devote considerable attention to the problems of "truth" in autobiography.[16] Having the author's psychoanalyst available certainly is one unique way to include some external verification of the events described and their psychological significance. I do not mean that the analyst's account is necessarily "truer" than

13. Schreber, *Denkwürdigkeiten eines Nervenkranken*, p. 388.
14. Marguerite Sechehaye, *Autobiography of a Schizophrenic Girl*, trans. Grace Rubin-Rabson (New York: Grune & Stratton, 1951).
15. Sigmund Freud, *New Lectures in Psychoanalysis*, quoted in Sechehaye, *Autobiography of a Schizophrenic Girl*, p. x.
16. Roy Pascal, *Design and Truth in Autobiography* (Cambridge, Mass.: Harvard University Press, 1960).

the patient's, but at least it is one additional account by a trained observer with honest intentions. Sechehaye gives her corroborative version of the factual events and behavior narrated by Renée, her view of the vicissitudes of progress and regression in the treatment and relationship, and her own growing awareness of what works in therapy. The book thus becomes a specialized form, the autobiography of a helping relationship.

In 1940 the *Journal of Abnormal and Social Psychology* published a series of autobiographical statements by academic experimental psychologists who had been psychoanalyzed.[17] I find these statements to be generally disappointing, although perhaps they were quite adventurous for American academic psychology vintage 1940. Nevertheless, this collection is of interest, especially because Edwin Boring's story is commented on by his analyst, Hanns Sachs. The problems of a successful, scientific, over-intellectualizing, achievement-oriented, emotionally isolated professor have a drama and pathos too, which is revealed as much as concealed by the author's attempt to maintain his façade.

Another scientist and intellectual has told a more revealing story of his psychoanalysis under the pseudonym of John Knight.[18] It is interesting to note that Knight's analyst requested him to narrate a brief factual autobiography at the start of treatment before embarking on free association.

During the course of treatment Knight's relationship with his mother improved greatly. At one point she tells him her own life story and what she knows of the family history. Knight finds this conversation deepens his bond with his mother and gives him an increased sense of his own identity. Here again, the sharing of autobiographical material can initiate a rewarding interpersonal interaction, rather than remaining a solitary act of self-analysis and ventilation.

I Never Promised You a Rose Garden, by Hannah Green, another autobiography by a patient, is an especially impressive

---

17. American Psychological Association, *Psychoanalysis as Seen by Analyzed Psychologists* (1953). Compiled and reprinted from the *Journal of Abnormal and Social Psychology* 35, nos. 1–3 (January–July 1940).

18. John Knight, *The Story of My Psychoanalysis* (New York: McGraw-Hill Book Company, 1950).

tribute to a psychotherapist and to the process of therapy.[19] The
authentic portrayal of Deborah's schizophrenia and her cure
would be almost impossible for someone who has not been there,
and is of great value to therapists such as myself struggling with
difficult therapeutic relationships.

Autobiographies by Psychotherapists

We have seen that autobiographies by patients frequently include
detailed descriptions of their therapists. Autobiographical writings by therapists themselves are also available to give us first-
hand views of the treatment process and/or the personal and
career development of the writers. Let us go back to Freud himself. Freud was extremly ambivalent about self-disclosure, and
we are left with no one consistent or comprehensive autobiographical portrait of him. In his writings on psychoanalytic
theory he frequently used himself for illustrative case material,
so that his *Interpretation of Dreams,* for example, includes analy-
ses of about thirty of his own dreams. On other occasions he
described "patients" who were really himself. From these fragments we could piece together one view of Freud.

A second view could be based on his published letters, especially the personally self-revealing ones to his financée Martha.[20]
Letters to one's fiancée, of course, have a purpose rather different
from autobiography, but Freud often described and reflected
upon his unfolding life because he was eager to share it with
Martha in order to bridge the long separations that preceded
their marriage.

A third view of Freud is in *An Autobiographical Study* written by him in 1923 at age sixty-seven.[21] No reference is made to
aspects of his life available in the other two sources, such as
his dreams or his close personal relationships. Instead, it is an

19. Hannah Green, *I Never Promised You a Rose Garden* (New York: Holt,
Rhinehart and Winston, 1970).
20. Sigmund Freud, *Letters,* ed. Ernst L. Freud, trans. James Stern and
Tania Stern (New York: Basic Books, 1960).
21. Sigmund Freud, *An Autobiographical Study* (New York: W. W. Norton
& Company, 1952).

"official" autobiography of an eminent scientist, with the same selective focus and omissions noted earlier in similar books. This is partly due to the circumstances under which it was written, always an important factor: it was published in a book describing the present state of medicine as revealed in the autobiographies of outstanding members of the medical profession. The translator, James Strachey, calls it an "auto-ergography," by which he means the story of one's work. And it may be that when Freud wrote it his life consisted primarily of work. Fromm asserts that Freud was obsessed with achievement to the detriment of close personal relationships and had distanced himself from his wife. Freud's own words seem to verify that: "Two themes run through these pages, the story of my life and the story of psychoanalysis. They are intimately interwoven. This autobiographical study shows how psychoanalysis came to be the whole content of my life and rightly assumes that no personal experiences of mine are of any interest in comparison to my relations with that science."[22]

This is certainly an unusual statement for a man who was continually demonstrating the multiple determinants of thought and behavior and the interrelationships among emotional, interpersonal experiences and intellectual processes. But the world had not been kind to Freud, and after all his battles it is understandable that he might be reluctant to risk further personal disclosures. For years he led the way in extending the range of our openness about ourselves. Owing to his work, all future autobiographies would be judged in terms of their psychoanalytic sophistication. Simple, idealistic, rational self-portrayals would never again be acceptable as adequate autobiography. Perhaps it is too much to ask that Freud be the first to live up to the new level of self-awareness and self-disclosure he helped make possible.

In a postscript written at age seventy-nine, four years before his death, as Europe was disintegrating, Freud concluded his autobiography as follows:

> And here I may be allowed to break off these autobiographical notes. The public has no claim to learn any more of my personal

22. *Ibid.*, p. 136.

affairs—of my struggles, my disappointments, and my successes. I have in any case been more open and frank in some of my writings (such as *The Interpretation of Dreams* and *The Psychopathology of Everday Life*) than people usually are who describe their lives for their contemporaries or for posterity. I have had small thanks for it, and from my experience I cannot recommend anyone to follow my example.[23]

Regrettably, Freud's pessimistic warning has generally been heeded by his successors, with a few fortunate exceptions. Theodor Reik, himself analyzed and taught by Freud, is one of those exceptions, and he chastises his colleagues for their reticence, especially regarding dreams:

I really believe that the fact that research in dream psychology remained so unproductive over the last 25 years is due to the relutance of psychoanalysts to interpret and to publish their own dreams. It is as if we ourselves were too—shall I say—cautious to talk about what we dream and what we discover about ourselves in interpreting our dreams. The instances in which analysts have published interpretations of their own dreams since Freud's lectures can be counted on the fingers of two hands. It's not easy to understand why we, who should know better, observe here the better part of valor. Demanding moral courage and sincerity from our patients, are we not obliged to set them a good example? No double standard should exist here. If our self-revelations were to discredit us in their eyes, then we have never deserved the credit they willingly give us. And if we were to disgrace ourselves by talking about our unconscious processes, then we have been in their good graces only through a mistake that must be rectified.[24]

Reik wrote *Listening with the Third Ear* in 1947 after thirty-seven years of analytic practice. The subtitle is *The Inner Experience of a Psychoanalyst,* and that is exactly what Reik conveys. He presents numerous examples of self-observation and self-analysis drawn from his dreams, his everyday life, and his work with patients. He traces the sequence by which he gains access into his own unconscious and uses that awareness in doing psychotherapy and in living his own life.

23. *Ibid.,* p. 139.
24. Theodor Reik, *Listening with the Third Ear: The Inner Experience of a Psychoanalyst* (New York: Farrar, Straus & Company, 1948), p. 37.

Allen Wheelis, a San Francisco psychoanalyst, has become one of the most noteworthy current successors to Freud and Reik's tradition by writing quite frankly of his formative years and ongoing experience. His book *The Quest for Identity* is appealing and unusual in that it alternates theoretical chapters with ones depicting the difficult childhood events that were the raw material leading to his theories. Wheelis has also written a novel, *The Seeker*, and while I have no idea how closely autobiographical it is, the protagonist is a psychoanalyst who lives out in fiction many of the conflicts Wheelis confronts in his other writings. A more recent book by Wheelis, *The Illusionless Man*, contains some autobiographical stories and two explicitly self-revealing pieces.[25]

The late Franz Alexander, another eminent psychoanalyst, was asked to write a concluding paper evaluating the autobiographical statements by the psychoanalyzed academic psychologists mentioned earlier.[26] As part of his review he submitted an autobiographical sketch describing the history of his own slow, resistant movement toward the field of psychoanalysis.

His father was a university professor for more than fifty years and represented the best of the traditional academic dedication to the arts and philosophy. Alexander chose to study medicine partly as a rebellion and became involved in physiological research.

He knew that his father was "thoroughly disappointed at seeing his son become a little compulsive laboratory worker, concerned with the decimals of oxygen consumption and blood acidity, forgetful of the essential problems of man, the broad perspectives, and the creations of the great geniuses in which man comes nearest to God."[27]

Working in a hospital, Alexander came in contact with schizophrenic patients. He attempted to understand them by rereading Freud's *Interpretation of Dreams*, a book he had previously

25. Allen Wheelis, *The Quest for Identity* (New York: W. W. Norton & Company, 1958) ; idem, *The Seeker* (New York: Random House, 1960) ; idem, *The Illusionless Man* (New York; W. W. Norton & Company, 1966) .
26. Franz Alexander, "A Jury Trial of Psychoanalysis," in *Psychoanalysis as Seen by Analyzed Psychologists*, American Psychological Association.
27. *Ibid.*, p. 308.

dismissed as "crazy." He talked with a young psychiatrist-pupil of Freud's and noted that "it became obvious that the patients with whom she dealt simply ignored the rest of the staff. Instinctively they felt that here was someone who understood their problems and dealt with their real issues."[28]

Alexander pursued his study of Freud, but was repelled by the idea of becoming a member of the scorned minority group that was the fate of psychoanalysts. Nor did he want to give up the promising academic career for which his own efforts and family tradition had prepared him. Finally, as is the case in the life histories of many great men, he had to resolve his feelings about opposing his father. "The practice of psychoanalysis was simply a horror in the eyes of the philosopher father, an undignified and morbid interest in the morbid. For this admirer of the highest aspirations of man, interest in sexual phenomena, not to speak of their pathological manifestations, was simply a descent into a spiritual gutter."[29] Alexander persisted, however, and his story concludes with a moving account of how his father finally came to value his son's new field, wrote a paper on it, and died with a copy of the *Psychoanalytic Almanac* open on his night table.

This brief autobiographical sketch by Alexander contains many of the basic ingredients found throughout autobiography. He describes the cultural milieu and the field of interpersonal forces into which he was born; his positive and negative reactions to these factors; his guilty, faltering attempts to establish a unique identity; his fear of rejection and isolation; his discovery of emerging strength within himself and in a new approach to life; his moments of truth when he confronts the opposition; his sense of triumph and integrity as he becomes his own man; and his happiness at making peace with those he had to oppose but did not wish to destroy.

Two other therapists deserve mention for their contributions to the new psychology of self-disclosure even though neither has published an autobiography. Carl Rogers and Sidney Jour-

28. *Ibid.*, p. 311.
29. *Ibid.*, p. 313.

ard advocate more openness by therapists, and their theories give central importance to the value of making oneself known to others. Rogers, for example, was one of the first therapists to publish verbatim typescripts of sessions with patients. He initiated a trend that has opened up to research the basic data of psychotherapy. His style of communicating to individual patients, groups, and students attempts to convey his own inner experience in ways that will resonate with others.

In the beginning of his book *On Becoming a Person* Rogers describes two lectures he gave to students about his own life. He comments: "the response to each of these talks has made me realize how hungry people are to know something of the *person* who is speaking to them or teaching them."[30] With this in mind, he begins his book with a brief chapter entitled "This Is Me," describing his development as a psychologist. What Rogers does tell us of himself in this chapter and here and there throughout the book makes us hope that some day he may produce a comprehensive autobiography. It would be a logical fulfillment of his belief that "what is most personal is most general."

Sidney Jourard's book *The Transparent Self* is subtitled *Self-Disclosure and Well-Being*.[31] It's an excellent basic statement of the author's hypothesis "that man can attain to health and fuller functioning only insofar as he gains in courage to be himself among others." "Full disclosure of the self to at least one other significant human being appears to be one means by which a person discovers not only the breadth and depth of his needs and feelings, but also the nature of his own self-affirmed values."[32] Jourard opens his preface by pointing out that "a choice that every one of us at every moment has is this: shall we permit our fellow man to know us as we now *are,* or shall we seek instead to remain an enigma, an uncertain quantity, wishing to be seen as something we are not."[33] He addresses himself to the questions

30. Carl R. Rogers, *On Becoming a Person* (Boston: Houghton Mifflin Company, 1961), p. 3.
31. Sidney M. Jourard, *The Transparent Self* (Princeton, N.J.: D. Van Nostrand Company, 1964).
32. *Ibid.,* p. 27.
33. *Ibid.,* p. iii.

of trust and the conditions under which we will disclose ourselves to another. Jourard believes that "no man can come to know himself except as an outcome of disclosing himself to another person."

Publication of one's own life experiences as a foundation for communicating one's psychological theory is strikingly illustrated by Viktor Frankl's *Man's Search for Meaning*.[34] Originally titled *From Death Camp to Existentialism*, the book is an introduction to logotherapy, Frankl's version of existential analysis. It is indeed fitting that the preface was written by Gordon Allport, who for years was one of the few exponents in this country of "the use of personal documents in psychological science." Allport wrote a book by that title, and the preface is dated October 1941.[35] He made a strong case then for the value of personal documents, but could hardly have known that, as he wrote, the Nazis were setting the scene for one of the most powerful such documents in the history of psychology. Frankl gives us ninety-three pages of his vivid personal experience in concentration camps, and then in the remaining forty pages sets forth his basic concepts of logotherapy. It is interesting to speculate on what education would be like if more theory were this integrally connected with the life and death struggles it grew out of.

The psychological uses of autobiography, both the writing and the reading of it, are numerous, and it is my hope that as psychology becomes more humanistic, autobiography will play an increasingly important role.

34. Viktor E. Frankl, *Man's Search for Meaning* (Boston: Beacon Press, 1963).
35. Gordon W. Allport, *The Use of Personal Documents in Psychological Science* (New York: Social Science Research Council, 1942).

Minor White

—————•—————

Extended Perception
through Photography

*When people talk about the uses of the arts in relation to psychology
or personal growth they generally mean dance, painting, perhaps sculpture or poetry. The art form most overlooked is the one most practiced
in America—photography. Almost everybody has taken pictures at
one time or another, and certainly they are a ubiquitous part of our
environment. Yet most of the taking of photographs and the looking
at them is a rather frantic business, with little real thought for the
power of the medium. Minor White, photographer and teacher of
photography, looks at the art as an approach to deepened personal
awareness and suggests a way of taking pictures and looking at them
that is closely akin to meditation.*

This essay contains outlines for three practical ways to extend
perception through photography. All three are related to the
canon of creative photography, "Be still with yourself." One
relates to looking at photographs, one to making them, one to
sharing with others responses to photographs.

First, however, let us meander into one of the peculiarities of
the medium, namely, that photographers and members of their
audience can be equally creative.

If cameras are for seeing, photographs are for looking.

If photographers can use the camera to extend perception
during the period called "making exposures," viewers or mem-

SOURCE: From *Ways of Growth: Approaches to Expanding Awareness*
edited by Herbert Otto and John Mann. Copyright © 1968 by
Herbert Otto and John Mann. Reprinted by permission of Grossman
Publishers.

bers of the audience can extend their own perception during the period called "looking at photographs." If there is anything creative here (and where else does creativity lie in photography?), then seeing and looking are equally creative. That is, the audience can be as creative as the photographer, and in virtually the same way. The "exercises" outlined in this essay are devised to demonstrate the similarity.

If in the process of extended perception the photographer makes contact with the essence of what he is about to photograph, the viewer may make contact with the essence of the image. That is, both open themselves to any suggestions that originate in the essence by deliberately inducing a state or condition called "extended perception." In academic circles the condition is called "heightened awareness"; in today's slang, "turned on."

If the photographer may bring about a state of heightened awareness by his own efforts, *the member of the audience may also make deliberate efforts to make contact with images.* Audiences have been blatantly spoon-fed for so long that they have become a visually illiterate society. Until members of the audience become willing to make efforts to *look,* they will never realize that one of their nagging hungers comes from visual starvation.

If a photographer can share his experience of truth or beauty through photographs, members of an audience can share with others their *responses* to the same qualities in images.

If photographers can take a responsibility for their images, members of a group can be equally responsible for their responses communicated to each other. Perhaps more than any other point, it is this last that caused the writing of certain exercises. (And the "exercises" may grow into a way of life for some readers.)

Extension of Perception by Looking at Photographic Images

The Simplest Exercise Possible

Select a photograph that you can look at for a long time with pleasure. Set aside some time, a half hour or so, that may pass without a single interruption. Set the picture in good light and yourself in a comfortable position. Look at the picture for at least ten minutes without moving even one small muscle, or "giving in" to even one tiny twitch. Keep your eyes and mind on the image, instead of following long chains of associations; keep coming back to the picture. You can expect that many things will be found in it, not previously noticed. After ten or fifteen minutes, turn away from the picture and recall what you have experienced, step by step. Make this as visual as possible; review the experience visually rather than with words. After the thirty minutes have elapsed, more or less, and the experience has become a kind of flavor, go about the day's work, trying to recall the taste when you can.

No one can predict what you will experience. The trick is to accept whatever the experience is for *what it is*. Then one will face a moment of truth, tiny though this moment may be, relative, limited or even negative and unexpected. It is only when one anticipates explosions, ecstasy, breakthroughs, thundering visions, that an actual, real moment of truth will be overlooked and therefore missed. If you habitually bring the notion of God into your activities, listen for the whisper. To our weak perceptions even thunder may reach us but faintly.

Elaboration of the Simple Exercise

The exercise above can be elaborated as far as one wishes. A model of one elaboration follows. It is for persons who are willing to prepare themselves and to make efforts to look at photographic images either alone or with others. The exercise is also for the photographer in his periodic role of audience to his own pictures, also by himself or in the company of others.

There are four stages, each with a few steps: *Preparation, Work, Remembering,* and *To Share*. That is, (1) becoming still with oneself in order to make contact with a *worthy* photograph, (2) working in a self-induced state of stillness of a special kind that engenders active perception, (3) the return to the usual state while remembering the visual experience or journey, and (4) sharing sometime later with others the interaction between image and self. The last stage really works best in company; hence we will treat the "to share" stage as a separate exercise in looking at images, for several people at once.

PREPARATION

The selection of a photograph has a bearing; so choose one that you like but suspect there is more present in than you have found so far. Photographs of water, snow, ice or clouds are fine to start with.

By being still you can make yourself voluntarily receptive to the suggestions coming from the image.

Remember that being still with yourself is a phenomenon possible in man which is an invitation to the unconscious to well up into the conscious. By being still with yourself you can help the wisdom of the psyche to infiltrate the commonly conscious mind.

Place the photograph in good light. Plan to hold it either in the hand or on a chair or other support. Seat yourself directly in front of the picture, *erect* and comfortable. It is of considerable wisdom to make certain that no interruptions will occur that might disturb your efforts.

Be prepared to postpone judgment of "good," "bad," "like," "dislike," until much later. The actions that these words call up, if allowed to remain in the mind while working with the picture, destroy any possibility of extension of perception.

Preparation continues by closing the eyes and starting to relax in a specific progression. Start by relaxing the muscles around the eyes, then the muscles of the whole face, then the shoulders, upper torso, and arms, letting the arms and body begin to feel buoyant as the relaxation progresses. Next relax the lower body, the thighs, the legs, and finally the feet, always allowing and encouraging the whole body to become buoyant and receptive. A more or less weightless body is ready for impressions of all kinds.

During this relaxing period the body will have been motionless; and in the three, four, five minutes that elapse energy will have collected that the body usually dissipates by needless and heedless movements. This energy becomes available to the mind as it is about to cross the threshold of perception, and the mind needs additional energy for just this purpose of perception.

Relaxing is purposefully directed from eyes to feet, while, on the contrary, the gathering of energy is deliberately directed from feet and hands to head. As the energy begins to activate the mind, prepare yourself to project some of this energy to the photograph and be further prepared to sustain such projection of force.

When you feel that there is abundant energy, open your eyes. The first flooding of the eyes with the image is a crucial moment. Your energy is projected as force without a shape; the image gives the energy a form and bounces it back to you with a shape. Furthermore, at this moment the "total image" may or may not be perceived by the "whole man" in a single strong impression.

Sustain that first strong impression. It may be necessary to close the eyes quickly to retain it. When you have a grasp on that impression, re-engage the image. What follows, that is, *the work period,* may be said to consist of your efforts to bring into the ken of the conscious mind what the psyche in the unconscious found in the image. In most humans it is as if a kind of "forgetter" is wired into the circuit between psyche and conscious mind.

WORK PERIOD

The work period may be held as long you wish or are able. The work consists mainly of overcoming the effect of the aforementioned "forgetter." The fact that a work period has arrived may generally be recognized from a certain clue. When the perception of space in depth within the image suddenly increases, one is in a working state. Some persons, however, experience other changes in the image, an increase of overall brightness or a change in size, usually larger, or a brightening of colors, and so on. This clue usually occurs shortly after the eyes are opened, and sometimes almost instantly.

After the first impression has been solidified for yourself in some manner, the work can start. Start active work by scanning the image in narrow bands: top left, across, and then back. Go back and forth until everything in the photograph has been seen and noted. Next scan the image according to the suggestions of flow and direction and relationships within the whole photograph. This is to make sure that you have seen all the relationships. When everything has been observed, start to study the images with whatever "tools" you can bring to the experience

—tools such as previous knowledge of design and composition, the techniques and composition peculiar to photography, the philosophy and metaphysics of image-making regardless of media, the knowledge of the subject from either long acquaintance with humanity or specialist knowledge of the subject photographed.

In addition you can also let associations flow—flow on and on, far away from the image at hand, and into the personal body of compulsions at that moment prevalent in yourself. The associations that flow up in you while looking at photographs seem to originate in the images themselves, but actually the associations originate in yourself. Consequently the associations that flow while looking at what are frequently called "abstract" photographs or any otherwise ambivalent images transform the photograph into a self-mirror. And the strangeness that arises in such instances is not a function of the image so much as a fact of yourself.

The photographic image as a mirror of the self is a contemporary experience. Oliver Wendell Holmes, literary American of the last century, once called the photograph a mirror with a memory. He referred, however, to the photographic record of the scene, which the camera does superbly well. For many members of society today the ambiguous photograph functioning as a mirror asks the man to remember himself. The ambivalent (that is, suggestive of more than one meaning) photograph can mirror the angel in us, the demon, the goblin, the saint, the matriarch, the harlot, the child, or the man, whatever is uppermost at the time. In a long work period, in a state of stillness, with ambivalent images, not only what is uppermost will surface into the conscious mind, but sometimes deeper hidden faces of ourselves will slowly drift into view.

The Passive Mode

Activity is not the only way to work in a state of stillness with a photograph or to remain sensitive to the suggestions that rebound from the image. Similar rewards may be anticipated if one remains passive. Sit in stillness, waiting, waiting patiently, without anxiety, waiting in readiness to receive suggestions and impressions; sooner or later the image will "speak" to you. It will even use your own words; how else, for who else is speaking? Some persons actually hear words. (This is the experience of the present writer.) Others hear colors, or sounds and music, or gestures, or other manifestations of the physical body. Whatever form the "speaking image" takes, the moment has the ring of conviction. A tinkle is about as much as the conscious mind can hear of the cosmic symphony, even when working in a state of stillness with both the self and the image.

To "turn on" the passive way, a certain word related to hearing helps some of us. This is the word "listen," and it is applied during an active work session. This does not mean to listen for sounds but to listen with the eyes to visuals or sights. The word is not to be taken literally, but allegorically. When this device works, the result is as if the sense of sight were relieved of the deficiencies of its own characteristics!

In due time, try both the active and the passive modes.

REMEMBERING

You may find that there is nothing new for you in these exercises. Most of us have experienced extended perception or concentration when something fascinated us, devoured our attention. The purpose here is to provide procedures and disciplines by which states of extended perception can be induced whenever one chooses, that is, by will and personal volition.

At the end of the work period the state of stillness is turned off. This is to be done on purpose, when you decide to. Both turning the state on and turning the state off are to be considered as great opportunities to exercise will. So choose to.

The return to our usual state of mental numbness and physical twitching is to be done in brief steps. Start by looking at the totality of the image; in other words, start to undo the spell by taking a final impression. Close the eyes, let the buoyancy out of the body, and it will soon move in its commonplace manner. Then turn away from the photograph and look elsewhere. Try very hard to hold onto the experience that has just been stopped. Try to hold on to it in silence, no words, not even to yourself. Review the various things seen, not as laundry lists, but as related visuals.

During this period of recalling the experience the intensity of the experience will diminish slowly or rapidly as the case may be, and the experience may begin to distill itself until only a taste or flavor is left. Even after the actual physical appearance of the image has disappeared, the "taste" of it may linger, and remain. The taste is amazingly persistent! If you are still compelled to judge something, evaluate the photograph from the taste. Judgment from "taste" has at least a slim chance of objectivity.

Though, I suppose, something like judgment must eventually be undertaken, what is more important than judgment and evaluation is tracing the effect of the image on yourself? Was some kind of change brought about? If so, where in you? Or what in you was affected? Was something added? Was something taken away? Was your energy dissipated uselessly, or gathered purposefully? And so on. Few enough images add anything to our inner life. The rest are millstones and albatrosses around our necks.

Images of any kind may be compared to physical food. When images add something or direct our energy to higher levels, they nourish us. Poisonous images are those that lead us into useless or frustrating stimulations or misinform or otherwise degrade us. Nourishing images are food of a special sort for something else in us. Most of the time we do not know whether a given image is poison or nourishment for this something. In states of heightened perception, viewing images in stillness, sometimes the person can realize which is taking place in him: something fine in him is being destroyed during an encounter with a photograph, or something coarse in him is being made finer. The wisdom of the psyche is able to distinguish.

Extension of Perception for Several People at Once

THE "TO SHARE" PERIOD

We may not want to share our intimate encounter with a photograph, especially if it has pushed a skeleton of ours into our face. Not all images can be expected to affect us this way unless, of course, our inner lives are almost exclusively a hodge-podge of skeletons and closets. More often when the interchange between ourselves and a photograph moves us, we have a considerable urge to tell someone. This urge to tell can be extended into a real communication with others, a communication that may be quite as effective as the photograph itself.

An exercise in sharing can be arranged easily enough. The preparation consists of gathering a small group of persons who have tried out the "simplest possible exercise" outlined above. One photo is quite enough for an evening's work. The following procedure is to be explained to everyone before the image is brought out.

After the picture is in place and each has found a comfortable place to view it, without any glare of light, each induces in himself the state of stillness of body and intensified activity of mind in the manner and steps described earlier. To facilitate working together someone should be charged with the duty of starting the relaxation, timing when to open the eyes and later to turn off the state of activated stillness. He will never be able to judge the various times required for each of the stages for each person, and so becomes something of a nuisance; but for group work everyone will have to bear with him.

It has been found that if the person charged with timing the successive stages uses certain phrases of a permissive nature, everything goes more smoothly. The points below may be used as a kind of check list to start. If the exercise is performed more than once or twice with the same people, abbreviations will arise of their own accord.

1. To start the relaxation period he may say, "After you have closed your eyes, allow the muscles around the eyes to relax." This is given in a quiet tone of voice.
2. When the coach thinks that everyone is relaxed, he can say, "When you are ready, encourage the energy to flow upward."
3. When he thinks that everyone is about to engage the photograph, he says, "Whenever you are ready, open your eyes." To help gauge the work period time, he notices when the last eyes are opened.

   (If there has been any hypnotic effect during this presentation period, from the moment the eyes engage the image all suggestions come from the picture.)

4. After about ten minutes have passed the coach can start the disengagement process with some such statement as, "That is probably enough for now." After a short pause of maybe a minute or so he gives the next directive.
5. "Whenever you are ready, take a last impression, close your eyes, and turn your head to one side."
6. When all heads are turned, "Let your body come back to its normal weight, and let it move as it usually does." This is said in a crisp tone of voice or manner of speech.
7. When all are stretching he adds, "Face your chairs away from the photograph."

The procedure outlined above should be explained (as was said) to all present before the session starts. It is especially important to caution members of the group to remain quiet and motionless after the head is turned away from the photograph, so that those who are still engaged in the photograph will not be disturbed any more than necessary. Actually, turning the head at this time is only a signal to the coach so that he will know everyone is through and bring the disengagement with the photograph to a kind of official close.

After the engagement with the image, the period of remembering is a private affair and is to be respected as such. Actively remembering, letting the experience distill into a taste, should be done in silence; and a relative quietness of body should persist for at least ten minutes. Because the group has met to share experiences and tastes, each member of the group will be expected to try to formulate during this period some way by which he can communicate to the rest his "trip": observations, understandings, or maybe the taste itself.

It should be arranged beforehand that approximately a ten-minute period will be given to this activity, and if no one has volunteered by then the coach can call on members.

To share experiences may prove to be a period of extended perception high in quality and of long duration. Someone of the group is likely to arrive at an understanding while he talks, and all will have their experience of the image enlarged. If each listens intently to the overtones as well as to the words, it may soon be realized that as each talks the spoken words are coming from a different place in the speaker than usual. The words may come out slowly, there may be a noticeable effort to speak, as if a translation from visual to verbal were in progress. These are all clues that a heightened awareness continues.

There is one type of occurrence to watch for during this period of sharing. As each person tries to tell what he saw while engaged with the photograph, almost every one of the rest will notice that the image seems to change and suddenly correspond to what is being pointed out. It is as if the image makes an actual move or transformation. Obviously the image does not really move or change; so the change must be in ourselves. Because we wrongly attribute the change to the image, we forget to look at what is really happening to us.

If we repeat the exercise with another photograph and with this event to watch for, as each person's experience "changes the image" we may get briefly the sensation that we are seeing with the eyes of the speaker. If so, the experiment will be worth the effort, because *for an instant at least we are given the opportunity to see objectively*, that is, to see with another person's eyes.

Gathering other people's responses to images, our own or those made by other photographers, can help us add to the meaning of individual images. As each person talks about his experience, our own journey through the photograph is enlarged. A question may be raised about the problem of everyone seeing something different in the photograph, and the familiar objection will come up, "But aren't photographs 'supposed' to convey just one thing to everyone?" So few photographs actually convey but one "meaning" that it is more realistic to accept the fact that everyone is going to get something different—and make the most of that reality. As one gathers responses from various types of people, the "image itself seems to grow" in meaning for everyone present. The opportunity to work with an image in the company of a few responsive persons is indeed rewarding and stimulating.

So important is "getting out of ourselves" and helping others do likewise, that communication of responses should be developed to the stature of a creative act in its own right.

THE RESPONSE

To help those who wish to undertake "sharing responses" for the first time, a few points to avoid or omit will be helpful. Omit the words *good, bad, like, dislike, ought, should* and *interesting* from the vocabulary of the group. Discourage obvious substitutes for these words. Avoid describing the image; everyone present can recall it. Recognize that one's prejudices at least color response and usually make response impossible. Curtail descriptions of long journeys that have ended in some pet compulsion that in turn has no bearing on the photograph. Look at the fact that each different response adds something to everyone's experience of the image. *Forget the popular cliché that photographs "should" mean the same to everyone. They do not; people are too varied.* In a group the experience of images is enlarged in a way that can happen in almost no other situation. When the photographer of the image being studied is present, his own concept of the image can also be enlarged, altered, and magnified—that is, if he is willing to accept the truth of a response and not throw out all responses that do not agree with his notion of what his image evokes or communicates.

To further help the people who will undertake sharing responses, we must clearly define both what is included in and what is excluded from this word "response." A "response" differs from a "criticism" in that it describes the journey or experience without evaluation of any kind. The journey may be delightful, oppressive, downright horrible, *all of which emotional evocations are simply treated as the facts of the journey and not evaluation of either the image or the person.* To exaggerate, a "response" is to be thought of as anti-criticism. A "response" is a fact; and no matter how limited the truth, that modicum of truth—"this is what took place in me"—is given in full confidence that no evaluation will be made by anyone present.

Sometimes to be able to speak freely of what one has experienced is an extension of the state of extended perception. Certainly each person's knowing that his "response" will be respected as a sliver of a truth will help him achieve a higher degree of awareness in the first place, and, better still, will assist the mode of extended perception to sustain itself during a period of sharing with others.

A "response" differs significantly from a "reaction," too. A *reaction is to be thought of as an accidental, uncontrolled, and unmanageable, more or less compulsive, happening that took place during the event of looking at a photograph.* A "response" is intended to indicate that a dialogue took place between you and the image—that is, if you are not overwhelmed by the image and so lose sight of yourself, but work as if with a colleague or a peer, and both parties are fully cognizant of each other, the image and the self in you. In other words, *something of yourself is recognized as present* in the interchange. This particular and special self-presence is something that will be particular to your response. And sharing with the group this special presence is exactly what members of the group can bring to each other in turn.

Visual Responses Instead of Verbal

For the sake of presenting the exercises with simplicity, responses have so far been treated as being only verbal. Actually, responses need not be verbal at all. If there is a dancer in the company, he can probably show something of his experience by making a gesture or a movement of the whole body. Any other dancer in the company will probably grasp the response in a specific way. A musically minded member of the company might go to the record collection and find a passage that corresponds to his experience. A painter or sculptor could dash off a sketch of his experience, and such a sketch need not be a simplified imitation of the photograph, but a new manifestation of his own private response.

Though most of us might not think so, all of us can make a workable sketch with a piece of charcoal pencil and a huge newsprint sketch pad. To demonstrate this, provide charcoal pencils and sketch pads to the members of a group, and at the sharing period have each person put down some kind of marks on the paper that correspond somehow to his experience. When they are completed lay them out on the floor for everyone to see. Probably most of the sketches will be rather meaningless. Here the person serving as coach can ask each person to explain with as few words as possible what the sketch stands for. Again, it is amazing and rewarding to see a meaningless few lines suddenly become the window into another person's mind and vision. The window also gives a view to the person's experience with the photograph. If there are experienced draftsmen in the group, often no words at all are needed. For those who may be putting pencil to paper for the first time since they were children, a few words will bridge the deficiency.

Extension of Perception at the Time of Photographing

Add a camera to the exercises previously tried out for looking at images. This exercise is best done with equipment that allows the photograph to be seen on the spot. Select an object: a branch of flowering dogwood, a chair, or an object that appeals to one and can be moved into comparative isolation. Have a hand-held type camera within arm's reach.

Set object and self into position similar to that used with an image. Prepare yourself to make contact with the object in the same manner used for making contact with an image; that is, relax, let the energy gather, and direct it into increasing mental activity, and then outward to the object when the eyes are open. The same kind of experience of increased sense of depth or other noticeable changes again indicate that a state of stillness is present.

Sit quietly, working actively by bringing everything you know or feel or sense into the act, or conversely by simply sitting quietly and completely open to any and all impressions the object might arouse. When you have felt somehow a resonance between your own life and the vitality or life of the object, contact is established.

Sustaining the contact, bring the camera into the line of sight between you and the object, and make an exposure. Slowly, very slowly, lower the camera while continuing the contact and while maintaining the state of stillness. The tendency here is to be so eager to see the results that the state of stillness is broken in the rush to operate the camera. This exercise is one that is intended to allow movement of the hands and arms while the state of contact is maintained with deliberate effort and the state of extended perception continues to exist. With plenty of practice one can learn, if one wishes, to sustain contact while making many exposures in a fast-moving situation.

When the operation of the camera during development of the picture demands looking at it, do so slowly, in order not to break the state of heightened awareness. Then study the photograph also in a state of extended perception. *A photograph made during a state of heightened awareness is frequently best seen in the same state,* by both the photographer and, as already pointed out, the audience.

Photographers reading this will have experienced that damnable gap between seeing and photograph. Closing this gap is a long, hard course in craftsmanship, that is, learning to see as a camera. Meanwhile, the photographer can slip into the role of audience and make "contact" with his own image as if it had been made by another person. Photography is so generous and so mechanical that often a photograph that fails the *seeing* proves to be an image on *looking* at it.

IMPLICATIONS FOR FURTHER EXTENSION

The various exercises are presented and intended to be used as starting points for future growth of the individual. Consequently, doing these exercises will suggest many other applications. For example, the efforts required and the state of stillness obtained to "make contact" with photographs may be extended at any time to include all kinds of objects, art, music, dance, and the more intangible world of thoughts and ideas. In fact, by the same methods one can make contact, by eliminating all thoughts and thinking, with the inner movements of forces and energies that go on in us all the time, but out of range of sight, hearing, taste, and so forth.

It is hoped that the reader has observed that this essay deals with the total movement of photography; and the exercises, if performed, might *involve* the performer with the same. This total movement is a complex interaction involving the separate elements of medium, photographer, subject/object, camera, and audience. The total movement unites these various elements and the various interactions with life-as-a-whole, when that in turn is in gear with the world of spirit-as-a-whole.

Roberto Assagioli

•

Pictures and Colors: Their Psychological Effects

*The late Roberto Assagioli, founder of the remakably eclectic school
of therapy called psychosynthesis, was a wide-ranging explorer who used
the insights of scientific psychology, literature and the arts, and the
religions of East and West whenever they offered usable insights into
the possibilities of human growth. In this short paper he discusses the
effects of visual stimuli—lines and colors—on the emotions of the
viewer.*

Pictures and objects of various kinds (paintings, drawings, and
all objects of art) often have a great suggestive power, especially
upon those who belong to the visual type. Their influence is
twofold: on the one hand, this is due to the intensity of their
expressive power or the charm of their beauty, and on the other,
to their inherent meaning.

This double combination explains the enormous influence of
works of art, an influence which has inspired millions of people
through all the ages and has often moulded a whole period or an
entire nation.

Thus, it would appear that in works of art there is much more
than mere aesthetic value; they constitute living forces, almost
living entities, embodying a power which has suggestive and creative effects. Therefore we should not allow this force to remain unused, or subject ourselves to it unconsciously and with-

SOURCE: From *Psychosynthesis* by Roberto Assagioli. Reprinted by permission of Psychosynthesis Research Foundation, Inc.

out definite purpose; instead, we should learn to use it deliberately for the further development of our personality.

To obtain the full benefit of this influence, it is necessary to observe the picture or object in the following way. We must contemplate it intently, in a state of sympathetic and quiet receptivity, and for a certain length of time, until we become wholly absorbed by it; until we feel ourselves to *be* the thing or picture we are contemplating.

For instance, if we look at the statue of Michelangelo's *Moses* (or even a reproduction of it), we should be able to *feel within ourselves* that wonderful, sustained power which permeates it. Or, if we contemplate the resurrected *Christ* of Fra Angelico, we should feel that it is *our own spirit* that has risen from the tomb; which has broken all bonds and is now free from all limitations, and manifesting as triumphant power radiating light around us.

To achieve these things, a certain degree of method is necessary, as in the case of making a collection of maxims and quotations from readings. We should collect and arrange a series of pictures, etc., expressing the quality or virtue we wish to acquire, using them *regularly* for that purpose and alternating them, when necessary.

Sometimes it is better to separate the different elements instead of using the combined influences of the chosen object; i.e., to take one portion at a time. For, though a single element is perhaps more restricted, it is also more concentrated and will help to bring about the desired result more quickly and effectively.

We can divide the elements into the following categories: (1) Lines and forms; (2) Colors.

Lines and Forms

It might surprise some readers to know that a mere line may have a denite psychological effect. But it is a fact, and some individuals feel these effects intensely and spontaneously. Many are more or less affected by them without being aware of it.

Straight lines, sharp angles, and broken lines produce very different impressions from curves, broad arches, and sinuous (wavy) lines. The former are, in a general way, suggestive of the masculine qualities, while curves and all their derivations are more expressive of the feminine characteristics.

Thus, the prevalence of straight lines gives the impression of firmness, hardness, decision, active and one-pointed energy; sharp angles turned upwards suggest aspiration and mysticism of an austere, transcendental type. It is typical of the pure Gothic style and of sharp, rocky mountains. Curves, generally speaking, suggest softness, breadth, expansion, rhythmical motion, change, plasticity, restfulness, kindness, love and passivity, and, in some cases, even sensuousness.

In architecture, we find curves predominating in the Baroque and Rococo styles, while Romanesque art represents the more harmonious blend of straight lines and curves.

In Nature, curves prevail in the watery elements; in the sea, with its rhythmic motion and endless waves, and in the clouds.

These general characteristics are sufficient to give us the key for the use of lines for different psychological purposes. If these principles were more widely appreciated and applied, then both the outer aspects of our buildings and their interior design would create a much more harmonious and helpful environment, intelligently adapted to our various needs and occupations. For instance, curves should provide the dominant note to places intended for rest and the pleasurable activities of social life, while the sterner, straight lines are more appropriate for places of work, such as factories, offices, and studios.

But we can use lines for psychological purposes also in their simplest and most elementary form, by just drawing a few lines on a piece of paper, or a single object of a certain shape, and then concentrating upon them. If we contemplate them in a receptive attitude, their influence will penetrate us and often awaken a response surprising in its directness and intensity. This offers us a very simple and pleasant method of achieving our aims.

The real connection between lines and their psychological qualitites is clearly revealed in our handwriting, and creates the basis of graphology or personality description through the study and analysis of handwriting. This offers another method of applying the above principles, for by deliberately changing our style of handwriting and adopting a style which expresses the qualities we lack, it will help us to cultivate those particular qualities. I know that definite results have been achieved in this way.

Colors

Colors have a more obvious effect upon many individuals and often a more powerful influence than lines.

It is generally admitted that each color has a distinct psychological quality of its own, and consequently a definite effect. There is still some diversity of opinion regarding the specific quality and effect of each color, and further investigation and experiments are still needed to give more light on this fascinating subject; but there are some points which can be considered as practically ascertained.

For instance, it is now generally accepted that so-called "cold" and subdued colors have a quieting effect, and that "warm," vivid, and bright colors have a stimulating or exciting influence. Certain shades of blue are usually considered as having a soothing, harmonizing effect; light green is refreshing; red and bright yellow are usually stimulating, while pink suggests serenity and happiness.

Miss Beatrice Irwin, author of *The New Science of Colour*, says:

Colour always has one of three effects upon us—sedative, recuperative or stimulating.

A colour is sedative when it has the power to induce contemplation, reflection, indifference, resignation, inception, coagulation, melancholy. It is recuperative when it can create conditions of change, balance, expansion, generosity, contentment, conception, cohesion. And stimulating colours are those which can excite hope, ecstasy, desire, aspiration, ambition, action, or which cau cause liberation of thought and emotion through achievement, dispersion, joy, peace, spiritual renewal and fresh growth.

The colors selected by women in their dress have a profound effect upon them, and usually satisfy (consciously or unconsciously) their psychological needs, besides exerting influence upon men who do not so express themselves. But perhaps the greatest scope for the influence of color is in the home.

The general principle for lines can be applied also to colors. Soothing colors are the best for places of rest and relaxation; bright, cheerful colors for private and public dining-rooms, clear or whole tones for places of work, etc. These are only general indications, but the principle can be adapted and varied according to the particular conditions and individual needs. Sunny rooms require different shades from those facing north, and, on a wider scale, the color tones necessary in southern climates differ from those better suited to the dull, cold climates of northern countries.

The influence of color as a therapeutic agent is also becoming increasingly recognized. I think in this respect it opens up great possibilities, but as a science it is still in its infancy and needs, as yet, to be used with much care. Even slight differences of shade and tone can produce widely different effects; much depends on the quality of the pigment used, and whether the color is reflected from a solid basis or background or is transmitted through a transparent medium.

The individual constitution and temperament of the patient is also an important factor. A color which mildly stimulates one person in a beneficial way can excessively excite another. Or a color which is agreeable and soothing in one case may not produce the slightest effect in others. Thus, much scientific experiment and accurate differentiation is needed, but the beneficial results well justify further research.* But, apart from these more thorough and systematic investigations, each individual can experiment for himself wth all these visual methods—pictures, lines, and colors. And each experiment can represent for us a pleasant and entertaining psychological game, with a resulting very definite gain for each one of us.

---

* We draw particular attention to the fine research work already carried out by R. Gerard of Los Angeles. See "Differential Effects of Colored Lights on Psychophysiological Functions," Ph.D. diss. (University of California, Los Angeles, 1958); "Color and Emotional Arousal," 66th Annual Convention of the American Psychological Association, Washington, D.C., 1958; *American Psychologist*, vol. 13, p. 340.

Janie Rhyne

•

The Gestalt Art Experience

In the preceding selection Robert Assagioli talked of the emotional impact of looking at art but did not proceed to any consideration of the experience of actively creating art. Janie Rhyne, an innovative art therapist, has developed processes for allowing people to create art, and to create it not so much for the traditional purpose of achieving a finished product as for the purpose of discovering what there is in the act of creation itself. The work is based on Gestalt therapy, which holds that the states customarily described as neurosis are marked by loss of awareness, an estrangement from feelings and parts of the self.

The sessions I lead are therapeutically oriented experiences in which the participants work with art materials to create paintings and sculptured forms as a means of becoming aware of themselves and their environment on a perceptual level. Although we use words to describe what we do and how we do it, the basic emphasis is on the preverbal, primitive level of immediate experiencing.

The approach is based on Perls's formulations of Gestalt therapy. My background training as an art therapist includes a self-designed academic program combining art, psychology, and anthropology, to which I have added several hundred hours of working as a participant in Gestalt therapy workshops led by various Gestalt-oriented psychotherapists.

SOURCE: Reprinted by permission of the editor and the publisher from J. Rhyne, "The Gestalt Art Experience." In J. Fagan and I. L. Shepherd (Eds.), *Gestalt Therapy Now*. Palo Alto, California: Science and Behavior Books, 1970.

Many people are curious about what we do in the art-experience sessions. Are we doing therapy? Are we creating art forms? Are we having fun? Are we playing games? Are we being childish? Are we acting like idiots?

My answer is that we are doing all of these. The activities or products may seem chaotic and meaningless, but they are related to the philosophy that knowing for one's self on the perceptual level is the most valid kind of knowing.

Most of the participants in the art groups function adequately in their living situations. Rather than therapy, they are seeking some added dimensions in their lives, such as increased self-awareness, enjoyment, or spontaneity.

I offer an assortment of art materials (clay, paint, glue, chalk) to an assortment of people (psychiatrists, nurses, social workers, hippies, middle-class suburbanites). I suggest that they use the experience of working with these materials to find out what they are feeling inside themselves. I also ask them to experiment with their senses and patterns of movement to find what message they want to give themselves, to trust their own inner awareness of what they want to express, so that they discover in themselves the capacity to create their own nonverbal symbolic language. Each person recognizes and interprets the images he makes in his own way. Some beautiful art forms emerge from this process, and some fearfully ugly ones. But aesthetics is irrelevant when we are working for self-discovery, and judgments of good or bad are eliminated as irrelevant. The question asked is, "What are you finding out for yourself?"

My job is not to analyze. The participants find their own answers in images and sometimes in verbalizing their private explorations to the group and to me. I am catalyst and facilitator, responding to movements, representations, and words. Although I have learned techniques to help people to get in touch with hidden areas of themselves, my best response is intuitive. I know that the best thing I can bring to my work is a sense of relatedness between me and the individual with whom I am working. When I go with him and feel with him, good things happen for both of us. When I am alienated from myself or he from himself, nothing valid happens to either of us.

The groups I lead vary in scheduling so much that even if I

wanted to, I could not work out a program or single procedure
to use consistently. Some groups are with me for only one evening,
some for a weekend; some spend several hours daily for a week
or more, and some come together once a week for a number of
months. The kinds of people who come are also varied—in their
backgrounds, ages, motivations, and general orientation in living.
I continue to be fascinated by the differences I see in these individuals and also by a deep communality that emerges when differences are not only accepted by the participants but are welcomed
as a way for each person to realize a wider comprehension of
the infinite range of variation among persons.

However, some of the groups consist of people who come together because of mutual interests and so bring a certain group
identity with them. For instance, I have worked with groups of
black teen-agers, young students from an experimental college,
the psychiatric staff of a university hospital, inexperienced psychiatric nurses in training, etc. Naturally, each of these diverse
groups has a sort of in-group personality with its own attitudes,
ways of verbalizing, and modes of self-expression which influences
the way I relate to it and the specific projects I propose. As much
as I can, I get the sense of the group and choose the techniques
I feel will be most effective for that particular constellation of
people at that time.

I respond to what I feel as being important happenings among
the participants and expect myself as well as each of them to be
flexible in how and what we do in any session. However, I have
designed a "process pattern," which I find a natural and effective
sequence of ways of exploration into each person's perceptual
awareness areas. The parts of the pattern develop as the process
of discovery takes place. When there is time enough, I encourage
people to use the art materials simply to find how and what they
can express graphically instead of verbally; they discover their
own vocabulary of forms and colors. Then, depending on the
amount of time available, we begin the process of exploring-
experiencing-expressing, with concentration on each person's
sensing of himself alone. Emphasis is on the ungrammatical but
essential awareness of *"This is me. I am."* In this phase, I stress
concentration on personal identity unrelated to environment or
others. I then propose a gradual progression of learning to in-

clude a perception of self in space, in time, in relationship to one another, in relationship with several others, and finally, in moving within the group in various environments.

In the process, I not only allow for but actively encourage times of regression and retreat into one's self. In a continuing group, the participants begin to create their own process, which develops in its own particular way. As this happens, I become less directive and act only as a catalyst and guide. Sometimes the group becomes essentially autonomous and needs me only to provide materials and suggestions for using the art experience to become more aware of what is happening. I am delighted when this takes place. I learn much from this process and feel free to become a participant myself, enlarging my own experiencing along with the others.

The eleven art experiences which follow illustrate the process I have described above. The reader is invited to make possible his own art experiences by carrying out any or all of the suggested procedures. Attempted or not, they give some indication of the kinds of experiences made possible through this approach.

Suggestions for Developing Your Personal Vocabulary of Seeing, Sounding, Moving

Have in front of you sheets of paper of varying sizes and shapes. If in a studio, have many kinds of chalks, crayons, pens, brushes, and paints that are yours to use. The studio should be large and secluded enough for you to move about and to be free to make any noises you want to.

And so, begin to find out for yourself your personal vocabulary for expressing yourself nonverbally.

The brilliantly colored chalks are coarse and dry. They fit into your fist and you can make bold lines and shapes.

The wax crayons are smaller and harder. The lines and forms you can make with them are shiny and slick, definite and clean.

The oil crayons are delicate and soft. You can blend them into rich tones that merge into one another.

The felt-tip pens contain watercolors. You can draw fluid lines and fill in clear, transparent areas.

With the paints, you can do almost anything; but they require more skill and take more time, so wait to use them until you have some knowledge of your own way of expressing yourself with form and color.

Do not decide what you are going to *try* to draw. Just go ahead and do what you feel like doing. Pick a color you like and move it around on the paper—scribble, doodle, let go of your trying. Make happy lines, tender lines, angry lines. Fill in shapes that express something you feel. Try different colors and various combinations of shapes. Recognize those that have some significance to you personally. Repeat those forms on other sheets of paper, not analyzing or even interpreting what meaning they have for you. Just be aware of how you are feeling when you make them.

You learn for yourself your own visual language; in creating your individual way of expression, you discover the messages you give yourself.

As you draw, begin making noises that seem to express the forms you are making. Don't use words—only sounds and only your sounds, the ones that feel natural to you. Don't stop drawing; let your sounds flow with your lines. You synchronize your visual rhythms with your vocal ones. Then, stop drawing and start moving your body in whatever way you find you want to, expressing what you have drawn and the sounds you are still making. Stand up and dance; lie down and roll; sit and rock; crawl, stomp, wiggle, leap, curl up—whatever movement seems to convey to you what you are feeling. Your movements are part of your private sensory language, and the sounds you make are your own way of saying something to yourself without wordiness.

Now, you are communicating nonverbally, with sights and sounds and movements, sending and receiving messages. *You are using your personal preverbal vocabulary.*

My nonverbal language changes as I change, and I discover it as I use it. To me, a bright clear red is noisy and a purplish scarlet moans quietly. Pale blue whispers; black is silent. Orange and yellow move toward me. Mauve retreats, and greens stay where they are. A line moving from the bottom of a page quickly upward has a rising inflection. If it goes off the page into space, it makes a noise like *"whoo-oo-oo-oop"*; a straight, broad band moving horizontally across a page hums quietly; a curved spiral sings its rhythm with a lilt; a lot of little dots and broken shapes chatter. A perfect circle and an unbroken sphere say something like "*om.*" A thick, dark, descending line groans heavily.

These are some my personal, subjective ways of perceiving sights, sounds, and motions all at once. When I draw or paint, I am putting some part of my sensing self into the process of discovering how I am communicating what I am aware of in myself. When I make noises, I am hearing myself sounding my feelings; when I move and become aware of how I am moving, I am experiencing myself as an instrument for expressing myself.

You have a preverbal language, too. Yours and mine are each unique to each of our personal selves; each of us has created a private vocabulary based on our individual ways of experiencing and perceiving. Ordinarily, we are not aware of using this kind of language in communicating with each other. Usually, we rely on the content of words to get across our thought to other people. We even talk to ourselves with words, either aloud or subvocally, carrying on a dialogue with ourselves. While we do this word-ing, we are not usually conscious that our silent languages are expressing how we really feel: Your handwriting indicates how you are feeling. The doodles you make are a way of saying something. The tone of your voice conveys messages beyond, and sometimes quite different from, the content of your structured sentences. Your gestures and body movements communicate your emotions.

Although each of us uses an individual silent language, we are not usually aware that we are giving and receiving communications that have nothing to do with words. But in this particular art experience, you do become aware of what you are expressing; of how you are *being* right then in the group. You show one another your drawings and listen to one another's sounds and see one another's movements. Your awareness of yourself and of others is more deeply felt and more explicit when you enhance your verbal ability to say what you think with the natural capacity to perceive and express how you *are* with your whole self.

Creating Your Self with Clay

Twelve people sit on the floor in a large circle, apart but facing one another. Hold in your hands a lump of clay. Let your palms and fingers feel the clay—cool, damp, slippery—a mass of dirt and water. With your hands, arms, and shoulders, weigh the clay. Move it from one hand to the other, getting the feel of it, balancing it, rolling it around as you will. Throw it lightly upward and catch it again. With your hands, explore how you can mold the clay, changing its surface, its texture, and its form. You can press, twist, squeeze, stretch, break, gouge, fold, smooth, scratch, caress—do all of these things to the clay and be aware of what you are feeling as you do them.

With your eyes closed, staying with your own feelings, fantasize as if you are dreaming—play a game with yourself in pretending *this lump of clay is you*. You can create your self by what you do to yourself. Do what you feel like doing, and feel what you like doing. Do not try to conceive of any representation of yourself or try to form any image of yourself. Let form or formlessness emerge or not as you make a record of your movements with the clay.

As your hands move, they will shape the clay. As you touch the surface of the clay, you will texture it. Be aware of the forms and tactual qualities of the clay as you feel them in relationship to you and what you do to yourself in living. If, in this process, a form grows and you recognize it as having personal meaning to you, let the form develop as it will, and let it change as you feel right with the changing. When you feel a sense of discovery and excitement, go with this excitement and create the form that feels like you. Open your eyes and see the form you have created. Be aware of your identity with it and of how much you can accept the clay as being an expression of *you*. As you look at your clay figure, relax your eyes, letting them become receivers of your image and your perception of yourself. Beginning with your eyes, relax your whole body. Lie down on the floor in a comfortable position and let yourself go on a fantasy trip. For these minutes, imagine that there is no one in the world but you.

What are you? You are not a simple, monolithic being. You are a complex structure, with many parts making up your whole.

Physically, emotionally, and spiritually you are continuously in motion within yourself. Every part of you is affected by every other part—you cannot separate your mind from your body from your soul. Your breathing affects your feeling, your thinking affects your breathing; when you feel fear, you become tense, you can't feel—when you don't trust your senses, you think so much you can't know anything that makes sense. All of these complex, interwoven patterns are you. You are a whole, too, functioning as a figure with the world around you as your background. You are a constellation in a galaxy. You are enough to make you dizzy. Allow yourself to be dizzy. Stop analyzing, stop thinking, and allow yourself to sense and *accept your being you as you are*—let yourself flow with yourself wherever your fantasies take you.

You may go far away and isolate yourself in your private world —wherever you are. In your own time, begin coming back into the world of here and now. Bring yourself back into the group. Open your eyes and see all the others around you. Be aware of each person in the room and receive what you can from each.

Speak to them of your experience in making your image only if you want to. Know, if you speak, that you can never, with words, describe the totality of your experience. At best, you can tell us only a condensed version. Sometimes, however, if you feel strongly about what you have done, your words, your tone of voice, perhaps your tears or laughter, may say it all. If not, and you feel frustrated at not being able to express what you experience, remember that the important thing is that you know what you are saying to yourself—that you recognize and accept as yours whatever you have done.

Your Self in Your Environment

Select from the varied sizes, shapes, and colors of papers provided, one particular piece you can imagine as representing you as you feel in your personal environment at this moment. Choose one drawing tool: pencil, crayon, chalk, paint, or even an ink-soaked rag that you can hold in your hand.

Sit where you will not be distracted by what the others are

doing or the sounds they are making. Concentrate for a few moments on the blank sheet of paper and be aware that you have chosen this particular piece to symbolize your personal environment. Is it large or small, square or rectangular, rough or smooth, light or dark? Consider your choice and what it may mean to you. Do the same with the drawing tool you selected. Take your time and give your imagination freedom to roam about in quiet awareness.

When you feel that you are using the right media and space, began simply and slowly by making one mark on the paper and consider its placement as representing where you are in your environment right now. In a corner? In the middle? At the bottom or top? Off to one side? Then, imagine this mark on the paper to be your center, and begin to extend its size, in any way that feels like you living from your center and in relationship to the boundaries of your chosen environment.

Do you stay small and simple, or do you spread out all over the page? Is the area too large for you or do you feel confined by too little room in which to be you? How do you feel as you enlarge the shape of you in your environment? Do you stay close to your center or leave it isolated while you wander all over the page?

Stay with your awareness of how and what you are doing, and do not judge or explain, even to yourself. Just find out for yourself how you feel yourself being in your present environment. Don't try to change anything. Just *know* for yourself where you are at this time in your perception of experiencing yourself as a figure on a background.

Your Lifetime

For this experiment you will need four rolls of paper of varying widths—six inches, one foot, three feet and four feet—and each hundreds of feet in length. You could spend many hours, maybe days, unrolling that paper and drawing on it, so for this experience I'd like you to fantasize that the length of paper in each roll represents infinity.

Choose which width of paper you want to use to draw and

paint on, and you can cut off as much length as you have a feeling for using. Before you make your choice, however, spend some time in a form of meditation. Get comfortable, close your eyes, and let yourself be cognizant of your concept of time in relationship to you. If you can, having realized how you conceive of time intellectually and abstractly, let go of those philosophical ideas; go into your perceiving of time as you *live* it. Time in itself neither begins nor ends; perhaps time curves, goes backward or forward, repeats, or stands still. I don't know what "it" does— and I don't think you do. So for now, forget "it."

We are all aware of our lifetime. I, as a process, a continuum of awareness, know time as *my lifetime*—passing, being, going. As I live in my time, I am involved with the consciousness of past-present-future. Let yourself, in fantasy, go into these areas. Wander around in your past, present, and future, and sense the space each has in your living and being. Don't try to understand, judge, or categorize your time sense. Simply find out for yourself how you live in *your* time.

Then choose a width of paper that seems right to you to draw on, and roll off as much length as you want, cutting off that amount of time-space for you to use in representing *your* temporal-spatial self. Use any medium and combination of techniques. Start anywhere on the paper and move in any direction. Divide the space into time areas as you feel like doing—or don't divide, if that's the way you see yourself living time.

In this experience, there are no rules for you to follow in expressing how you are living in time. Find out how you are living your lifetime and that's enough for here and now.

Use your drawing as a concrete reference when you talk to the group of how you are in your lifetime.

Use your art work as a bridge, communicating to yourself and to others some awareness of yourself in your lifetime which you know on a perceptive level but which you cannot express in words.

Your Self and an Other in Space

Sit facing a partner and between you place a large, blank sheet of paper and a basket of fist-size chalks of many colors. You and your partner look at each other directly for a time until you feel you have made contact, that on some level you know the other. Then, look at the paper between you; be aware of its spatial dimensions and realize that the space you see belongs to both of you; for now the paper represents an environment in which you two are being together. You both draw on the one sheet at the same time, discovering, as you do, what you feel in sharing your relationship with the other within that space. Using lines, shapes, and colors, you can communicate in many ways. Using no words, you can demand space to be left alone in; you can push your partner into a corner; you can share some areas or the whole page; you can go toward or retreat from each other; you can support, cross out, cover up, cooperate with, oppose, lead, or follow your partner. Your possibilities for nonverbal interaction are limitless.

When you both feel that you have finished your graphic communicating, talk awhile with each other, finding out how explicitly you gave and received your messages. Then, change partners, and repeat the process.

You are representing graphically on a simple, primitive level your perception of territoriality and how it affects and is affected by your relationship with another person.

An Other Who Is Also You

Take in your hands a large amount of clay and hold it for a while, moving the mass with your hands, letting them express what you are feeling without trying to be explicit, even to yourself, about what your hands are doing. Close your eyes and gradually focus your awareness on some person with whom you have deep emotional ties, someone primary in your ways of responding to life. This person may be miles away; you may not have had any contact with him for years; he may be physically dead; he may, perhaps, exist for you only in your fantasy life. Choose to concentrate on someone who is so much with you on an emotional level that you are unaware, on a conscious rational basis, of what part of you is this other, and whether or not you perceive the other at all, except as a part of you.

Find out, using the clay to make explicit for yourself, how you can form an image of this other as you perceive him to be. Be aware of how much of you is *your* imagery. How much of your emotional energy is invested in this other? Do you know experientially who the other *is*, apart from you? Can you separate his "is-ness" from your own? Is this other also you? Are you making an image of a disowned part of yourself?

Explore and discover your awareness as you work with the clay. Ask yourself the questions that seem relevant to you in this area and find your own answers.

Giving Attention to Another Person

Choose a partner from the group, arranging by mutual consent to be with someone you do not know very well. Maybe you are interested in this other person and curious to know him better; maybe you don't like him; maybe he seems so alien to you that you can't communicate at all. Choose and be chosen.

Each of you takes handfuls of clay and a small clay board on which to work. Sit down on the floor back to back with your partner, each of you placing your clay in front of you but not touching it for a while. Instead, touch your partner with as much of your back, shoulders, head, and arms as you two can agree on nonverbally. Do not look at each other; make contact only with your touching and your movements. Lean on each other; push backward and forward; find out how you move together and how you do not. Give full attention to sensing the other person as you feel him to be.

At a time when you, as partners, can communicate that you have reached some kind of recognition of the other, lean forward and begin working the clay into an image representing what impressions you have received from and with your partner in making contact only in this way. When you have finished the clay image, turn and face your partner and with the two clay figures between you, talk quietly and briefly with each other of how you've described your response in making your clay images.

Then, providing yourselves with paper and drawing tools, come back to your same partner and sit facing each other, without

touching, but close enough so that you can make contact with
your eyes. See each other with your eyes; discover as much as you
can of the other using your eyes as senders and receivers of
messages. Maintain this nonverbal relating as long as you both
want to, staying with each other until you feel you really are
with each other. Then, draw a portrait of the other as you know
him through his eyes. The portrait can be representational, abstract, or symbolic; whatever way you want and can do it. Again,
have a brief, quiet verbal conversation without going into detailed interpretations or explanations.

Now, try knowing the other through your hands. Touch and
explore your partner's hands. Move your hands together in whatever way you two find natural for you. Be aware of your own
feelings and desires and resistances, at the same time concentrating your attention on what your partner is conveying to you with
his hands. When you feel that you have reached a time for
terminating your contact, draw a representation of your experiencing him through your hands and his exploration of you.

Using all three images as references, speak now with each other
in any way you want to, using words, touching, drawing, movement, and perhaps silence. Let yourselves be with each other as
you can and want to be.

If you want to, and other partners agree, come together again
as a group and present each other to the group as a whole. If
there is time, change partners and repeat the sequence with
another, being aware of how you respond to each. Be especially
aware of how much you can know another being, unique, different, separate from you and at the same time *with* you in mutual
response, when you give each other your concentrated attention.

Creating a World That Is You

For this experience, you use collage and assemblage as art techniques that make it possible for you to put all sorts of materials
together in some way you identify as being *yours.* You can use
paper, wood, wire, leaves, stones—anything that you find and
want to use, and that communicates to you, "This is my world,
made by me, for me, with whatever I choose to use."

The simplest technique is paper on paper, using rubber cement or white glue to make an arrangement of different colors, forms, and areas. You can use colored papers, both opaque and semi-transparent; sections cut or torn from magazines, newspapers, wallpaper books; cardboard or parts of boxes. From a two-dimensional collage, you can build into a third dimension and make an assemblage. Or, you can begin with a structure which is a free-standing sculptural form or a mobile made to hang by wire from the ceiling.

Wander around for a while, in the studio and, if possible, outside, *seeing* what is available to you and being aware of your feeling of personal identification with materials and objects. You don't have to explain to yourself or to anyone else why you want to use some and not others. Choose what you feel like using and use them in any way you have a feeling for doing.

Perhaps you will want to show your worlds to each other and talk about them with the group as a whole. Perhaps not. The important thing is that you see your own world and recognize for yourself, "I structured this world with materials I chose; within the limits of what is possible for me, I take responsibility for creating my own personal world."

Accepting and Rejecting What Is Offered

Neither you nor I, in actuality, can choose entirely what will be in our personal worlds; we learn experientially in the living process that we must continually accept and reject from what is being offered to us by others. Each of us creates our own individual Gestalt by assimilating that which we can make a functional part of our own structure.

The next art experience can make you aware of how you feel and what you do when you let others put upon you anything they want to.

For this session, sit in a closed circle with one sheet of paper and felt-tip pens in many colors near you. Begin a drawing on your sheet of paper, starting but not finishing a graphic description of something important to you. At a signal, pass your drawing to the person on your left, at the same time receiving from the person on your right the drawing he has begun. See what this drawing means to you and work on it as if it were yours, adding and changing it as you want to. At the signal, pass this drawing to your left and receive another from your right, and so on around the circle until the drawing you began originally comes back to you.

You may not recognize it easily. What you put on the paper has been modified by what several others have put there. Your drawing may even be obliterated by those of others. But look at it and really see what is there on the page. Be aware of how you feel in seeing the expressions of others imposed on your own.

Is there anything of you left in that composite drawing? Is there anything which is not you, but which you'd like to keep? Are there areas you'd like to obliterate? What do you want to do with this pattern that is in your hands now? Using art materials, what can you do?

Be aware of your feelings and take some action that expresses them.

Making a World Together

Sit around a large paper circle that belongs to all of you. Place on it a pile of assorted stuff: odd shapes of colored paper, pieces of string, straw, beads, bits of wood and foam rubber.

Pretend that the circle is a space where you, as a group, can create a world, and that the materials on the circle are elements from which you can choose, to use in creating a Gestalt, a figure on and related to the background of *your* world—the world you make here and now among yourselves.

From the pile of materials on the world, choose individually what you want to use in representing *you* in the world. Remove these from the common pile and claim them as your own. When each of you has done this, make a group decision as to what you will do with the materials left on the world, which no one wants to use at the moment.

Provide scissors, crayons, and glue to work with. Use these tools and your materials to create a collage on the circle representing your interrelationships and how you are perceiving yourselves as *being* in one limited environment. Talk with each other as you work, use sounds to express your responses, move about the circumference of the world, but stay with and be active in making the world, unless you do not want to have any part in this activity. If you feel a need to withdraw, leave the room physically.

There are no rules as to what kind of world you create and how you go about it except those that evolve among you in the process of your working and being together as intensely as you can be. As you do this, be aware of your personal role in this process and your feelings of how much of what you are doing now you also do in your real-world living situation.

You are playing an imagery game that makes concrete and explicit your acceptance of yourself as an active creator of the world of process with many others—what we are each being and doing in an environment which is nothing in itself. With our capacities for awareness and our abilities for action, we make our own world out of materials available to us.

The representations we make of our perceptions of our ways of being in our world are "images" when we make them with art materials. This imagery can become a way of exploring, experiencing, and expressing what is not imagery—what is the reality of me and of you, speaking in the first-person singular in the present tense.

Moving Together

For this art experience, the most essential element is your own willingness to let go of your dignity and let happen what will.

You also need space—a big space to move in and a hard, rough surface to draw on. A tennis court is perfect; a wide sidewalk will do. Have several boxes of brilliantly colored chalks handy—the big, fat, fist-sized ones. Wear old clothes and go barefoot. When you finish, you'll be a mess, so have hot water and soap somewhere nearby.

With chalk in hands, all of you start drawing on the hard-surfaced area. Move as you draw and draw as you move. Make lines and areas, and make them big and flowing. Move together and draw together. Draw on each other. Celebrate together that we can be alive together when we are each ourselves. Enjoy.

Sanity and Madness
in the Arts

Lionel Trilling

———•———

Art and Neurosis

*One of the persistent notions that turns up in discussions about the
psychology of art is the idea that art can best be understood as a
symptom of emotional disturbance; the artist, in short, is crazy. This
idea, always popular in a culture that has tended to define health as
adjustment to the dull but respectable nine-to-five existence, has some
support from Freudian psychology and even—as Lionel Trilling notes
—from artists themselves, whose admiration for society's version of
sanity has never been overwhelming. Trilling argues here for a greater
appreciation of the strength and purpose involved in artistic creation
—a view that comes close to the ideas of Koestler and Maslow*

The question of the mental health of the artist has engaged the
attention of our culture since the beginning of the Romantic
Movement. Before that time it was commonly said that the poet
was "mad," but this was only a manner of speaking, a way of
saying that the mind of the poet worked in different fashion from
the mind of the philosopher; it had no real reference to the
mental hygiene of the man who was the poet. But in the early
nineteenth century, with the development of a more elaborate
psychology and a stricter and more literal view of mental and
emotional normality, the statement was more strictly and literally
intended. So much so, indeed, that Charles Lamb, who knew
something about madness at close quarters and a great deal about

SOURCE: From *The Liberal Imagination* by Lionel Trilling. Copyright
1945, Copyright © renewed 1973 by Lionel Trilling. Reprinted by
permission of The Viking Press, Inc.

art, undertook to refute in his brilliant essay, "On the Sanity of True Genius," the idea that the exercise of the imagination was a kind of insanity. And some eighty years later, the idea having yet further entrenched itself, Bernard Shaw felt called upon to argue the sanity of art, but his cogency was of no more avail than Lamb's. In recent years the connection between art and mental illness has been formulated not only by those who are openly or covertly hostile to art, but also and more significantly by those who are most intensely partisan to it. The latter willingly and even eagerly accept the idea that the artist is mentally ill and go on to make his illness a condition of his power to tell the truth.

This conception of artistic genius is indeed one of the characteristic notions of our culture. I should like to bring it into question. To do so is to bring also into question certain early ideas of Freud's and certain conclusions which literary laymen have drawn from the whole tendency of the Freudian psychology. From the very start it was recognized that psychoanalysis was likely to have important things to say about art and artists. Freud himself thought so, yet when he first addressed himself to the subject he said many clumsy and misleading things. I have elsewhere and at length tried to separate the useful from the useless and even dangerous statements about art that Freud has made.[1] To put it briefly here, Freud had some illuminating and even beautiful insights into certain particular works of art which made complex use of the element of myth. Then, without specifically undertaking to do so, his *Beyond the Pleasure Principle* offers a brilliant and comprehensive explanation of our interest in tragedy. And what is of course most important of all—it is a point to which I shall return—Freud, by the whole tendency of his psychology, establishes the *naturalness* of artistic thought. Indeed, it is possible to say of Freud that he ultimately did more for our understanding of art than any other writer since Aristotle; and this being so, it can only be surprising that in his early work he should have made the error of treating the artist as a neurotic who escapes from reality by means of "substitute gratifications."

---

1. See "Freud and Literature" [in Lionel Trilling, *The Liberal Imagination* (New York: The Viking Press, 1950) , pp. 34–58].

As Freud went forward he insisted less on this simple formula-tion. Certainly it did not have its original force with him when, at his seventieth birthday celebration, he disclaimed the right to be called the discoverer of the unconscious, saying that whatever he may have done for the systematic understanding of the un-conscious, the credit for its discovery properly belonged to the literary masters. And psychoanalysis has inherited from him a tenderness for art which is real although sometimes clumsy, and nowadays most psychoanalysts of any personal sensitivity are embarrassed by occasions which seem to lead them to reduce art to a formula of mental illness. Nevertheless Freud's early belief in the essential neuroticism of the artist found an all too fertile ground—found, we might say, the very ground from which it first sprang, for, when he spoke of the artist as a neurotic, Freud was adopting one of the popular beliefs of his age. Most readers will see this belief as the expression of the industrial rationalization and the bourgeois philistinism of the nineteenth century. In this they are partly right. The nineteenth century established the basic virtue of "getting up at eight, shaving close at a quarter-past, breakfasting at nine, going to the City at ten, coming home at half-past five, and dining at seven." The Messrs. Podsnap who instituted this scheduled morality inevitably decreed that the arts must celebrate it and nothing else. "Nothing else to be permitted to these . . . vagrants the Arts, on pain of excommunication. Nothing else To Be—anywhere!" We observe that the virtuous day ends with dinner—bed and sleep are naturally not part of the Reality that Is, and nothing must be set forth which will, as Mr. Podsnap put it, bring a Blush to the Cheek of a Young Person.

The excommunication of the arts, when it was found necessary, took the form of pronouncing the artist mentally degenerate, a device which eventually found its theorist in Max Nordau. In the history of the arts this is new. The poet was always known to belong to a touchy tribe—*genus irritabile* was a tag anyone would know—and ever since Plato the process of the inspired imagina-tion, as we have said, was thought to be a special one of some interest, which the similitude of madness made somewhat in-telligible. But this is not quite to say that the poet was the victim of actual mental aberration. The eighteenth century did not find the poet to be less than other men, and certainly the Renaissance

did not. If he was a professional, there might be condescension
to his social status, but in a time which deplored all professional-
ism whatever, this was simply a way of asserting the high value of
poetry, which ought not to be compromised by trade. And a
certain good nature marked even the snubbing of the professional.
At any rate, no one was likely to identify the poet with the
weakling. Indeed, the Renaissance ideal held poetry to be, like
arms or music, one of the signs of manly competence.

The change from this view of things cannot be blamed wholly
on the bourgeois or philistine public. Some of the "blame" must
rest with the poets themselves. The Romantic poets were as proud
of their art as the vaunting poets of the sixteenth century, but
one of them talked with an angel in a tree and insisted that Hell
was better than Heaven and sexuality holier than chastity; another told the world that he wanted to lie down like a tired child
and weep away this life of care; another asked so foolish a question as "Why did I laugh tonight?"; and yet another explained
that he had written one of his best poems in a drugged sleep.
The public took them all at their word—they were not as other
men. Zola, in the interests of science, submitted himself to examination by fifteen psychiatrists and agreed with their conclusion
that his genius had its source in the neurotic elements of his
temperament. Baudelaire, Rimbaud, Verlaine found virtue and
strength in their physical and mental illness and pain. W. H.
Auden addresses his "wound" in the cherishing language of a
lover, thanking it for the gift of insight it has bestowed. "Knowing you," he says, "has made me understand." And Edmund Wilson in his striking phrase, "the wound and the bow," has formulated for our time the idea of the characteristic sickness of the
artist, which he represents by the figure of Philoctetes, the Greek
warrior who was forced to live in isolation because of the dis-
gusting odor of a suppurating wound and who yet had to be
sought out by his countrymen because they had need of the
magically unerring bow he possessed.

The myth of the sick artist, we may suppose, has established
itself because it is of advantage to the various groups who have
one or another relation with art. To the artist himself the myth
gives some of the ancient powers and privileges of the idiot and

the fool, half-prophetic creatures, or of the mutilated priest. That the artist's neurosis may be but a mask is suggested by Thomas Mann's pleasure in representing his untried youth as "sick" but his successful maturity as senatorially robust. By means of his belief in his own sickness, the artist may the more easily fulfill his chosen, and assigned, function of putting himself into connection with the forces of spirituality and morality; the artist sees as insane the "normal" and "healthy" ways of established society, while aberration and illness appear as spiritual and moral health if only because they controvert the ways of respectable society.

Then too, the myth has its advantage for the philistine—a double advantage. On the one hand, the belief in the artist's neuroticism allows the philistine to shut his ears to what the artist says. But on the other hand it allows him to listen. For we must not make the common mistake—the contemporary philistine does want to listen, at the same time that he wants to shut his ears. By supposing that the artist has an interesting but not always reliable relation to reality, he is able to contain (in the military sense) what the artist tells him. If he did not want to listen at all, he would say "insane"; with "neurotic," which hedges, he listens when he chooses.

And in addition to its advantage to the artist and to the philistine, we must take into account the usefulness of the myth to a third group, the group of "sensitive" people, who, although not artists, are not philistines either. These people form a group by virtue of their awareness of their own emotional pain and uncertainty. To these people the myth of the sick artist is the institutional sanction of their situation; they seek to approximate or acquire the character of the artist, sometimes by planning to work or even attempting to work as the artist does, always by making a connection between their own powers of mind and their consciousness of "difference" and neurotic illness.

The early attempts of psychoanalysis to deal with art went on the assumption that, because the artist was neurotic, the content of his work was also neurotic, which is to say that it did not stand in a correct relation to reality. But nowadays, as I have said, psychonalysis is not likely to be so simple in its transactions with art. A good example of the psychoanalytical development in this respect is Dr. Paul Rosenzweig's well-known essay, "The Ghost of Henry James."[2] This is an admirable piece of work, marked by accuracy in the reporting of the literary fact and by respect for the value of the literary object. Although Dr. Rosenzweig explores the element of neurosis in James's life and work, he nowhere suggests that this element in any way lessens James's value as an artist or moralist. In effect he says that neurosis is a way of dealing with reality which, in real life, is uncomfortable and uneconomical, but that this judgment of neurosis in life cannot mechanically be transferred to works of art upon which neurosis has had its influence. He nowhere implies that a work of art in whose genesis a neurotic element may be found is for that reason irrelevant or in any way diminished in value. Indeed, the manner of his treatment suggests, what is of course the case, that every neurosis deals with a real emotional situation of the most intensely meaningful kind.

Yet as Dr. Rosenzweig brings his essay to its close, he makes use of the current assumption about the causal connection between the psychic illness of the artist and his power. His investigation of James, he says, "reveals the aptness of the Philoctetes pattern." He accepts the idea of "the sacrificial roots of literary power" and speaks of "the unhappy sources of James's genius." "The broader application of the inherent pattern," he says, "is familar to readers of Edmund Wilson's recent volume *The Wound and the Bow.* . . . Reviewing the experience and work of several well-known literary masters, Wilson discloses the sacrificial roots of their power on the model of the Greek legend. In the case of Henry James, the present account . . . provides a similar insight into the unhappy sources of his genius. . . ."

This comes as a surprise. Nothing in Dr. Rosenzweig's theory requires it. For his theory asserts no more than that Henry James, predisposed by temperament and family situation to certain mental and emotional qualities, was in his youth injured in a way which he believed to be sexual; that he unconsciously invited the injury in the wish to identify himself with his father, who himself had been similarly injured—"castrated": a leg had

2. First published in *Character and Personality*, December 1943, and reprinted in *Partisan Review*, Fall 1944.

been amputated—and under strikingly similar circumstances; this resulted for the younger Henry James in a certain pattern of life and in a preoccupation in his work with certain themes which more or less obscurely symbolize his sexual situation. For this I think Dr. Rosenzweig makes a sound case. Yet I submit that this is not the same thing as disclosing the roots of James's power or discovering the sources of his genius. The essay which gives Edmund Wilson's book its title and cohering principle does not explicitly say that the roots of power are sacrificial and that the source of genius is unhappy. Where it is explicit, it states only that "genius and disease, like strength and mutilation, may be inextricably bound up together,"which of course, on its face, says no more than that personality is integral and not made up of detachable parts; and from this there is no doubt to be drawn the important practical and moral implication that we cannot judge or dismiss a man's genius and strength because of our awareness of his disease or mutilation. The Philoctetes legend in itself does not suggest anything beyond this. It does not suggest that the wound is the price of the bow, or that without the wound the bow may not be possessed or drawn. Yet Dr. Rosenzweig has accurately summarized the force and, I think, the intention of Mr. Wilson's whole book; its several studies do seem to say that effectiveness in the arts does depend on sickness.

An examination of this prevalent idea might well begin with the observation of how pervasive and deeply rooted is the notion that power may be gained by suffering. Even at relatively high stages of culture the mind seems to take easily to the primitive belief that pain and sacrifice are connected with strength. Primitive beliefs must be treated with respectful alertness to their possible truth and also with the suspicion of their being magical and irrational, and it is worth noting on both sides of the question, and in the light of what we have said about the ambiguous relation of the neurosis to reality, that the whole economy of the neurosis is based exactly on this idea of the *quid pro quo* of sacrificial pain: the neurotic person unconsciously subscribes to a system whereby he gives up some pleasure or power, or inflicts pain on himself, in order to secure some other power or some other pleasure.

In the ingrained popular conception of the relation between

suffering and power there are actually two distinct although related ideas. One is that there exists in the individual a fund of power which has outlets through various organs or faculties, and that if its outlet through one organ or faculty be prevented, it will flow to increase the force or sensitivity of another. Thus it is popularly believed that the sense of touch is intensified in the blind not so much by the will of the blind person to adapt himself to the necessities of his situation as, rather, by a sort of mechanical redistribution of power. And this idea would seem to explain, if not the origin of the ancient mutilation of priests, then at least a common understanding of their sexual sacrifice.

The other idea is that a person may be taught by, or proved by, the endurance of pain. There will easily come to mind the ritual suffering that is inflicted at the tribal initiation of youths into full manhood or at the admission of the apprentice into the company of journeymen adepts. This idea in sophisticated form found its way into high religion at least as early as Aeschylus, who held that man achieves knowledge of God through suffering, and it was from the beginning an important element of Christian thought. In the nineteenth century the Christianized notion of the didactic suffering of the artist went along with the idea of his mental degeneration and even served as a sort of countermyth to it. Its doctrine was that the artist, a man of strength and health, experienced and suffered, and thus learned both the facts of life and his artistic craft. "I am the man, I suffered, I was there," ran his boast, and he derived his authority from the knowledge gained through suffering.

There can be no doubt that both these ideas represent a measure of truth about mental and emotional power. The idea of didactic suffering expresses a valuation of experience and of steadfastness. The idea of natural compensation for the sacrifice of some faculty also says something that can be rationally defended: one cannot be and do everything, and the wholehearted absorption in any enterprise, art, for example, means that we must give up other possibilities, even parts of ourselves. And there is even a certain validity to the belief that the individual has a fund of undifferentiated energy which presses the harder upon what outlets are available to it when it has been deprived of the normal number.

Then, in further defense of the belief that artistic power is connected with neurosis, we can say that there is no doubt that what we call mental illness may be the source of psychic knowledge. Some neurotic people, because they are more apprehensive than normal people, are able to see more of certain parts of reality and to see them with more intensity. And many neurotic or psychotic patients are in certain respects in closer touch with the actualities of the unconscious than are normal people. Further, the expression of a neurotic or psychotic conception of reality is likely to be more intense than a normal one.

Yet when we have said all this, it is still wrong, I believe, to find the root of the artist's power and the source of his genius in neurosis. To the idea that literary power and genius spring from pain and neurotic sacrifice there are two major objections. The first has to do with the assumed uniqueness of the artist as a subject of psychoanalytical explanation. The second has to do with the true meaning of power and genius.

One reason why writers are considered to be more available than other people to psychoanalytical explanation is that they tell us what is going on inside them. Even when they do not make an actual diagnosis of their malaises or describe "symptoms," we must bear it in mind that it is their profession to deal with fantasy in some form or other. It is in the nature of the writer's job that he exhibit his unconscious. He may disguise it in various ways, but disguise is not concealment. Indeed, it may be said that the more a writer takes pains with his work to remove it from the personal and subjective, the more—and not the less—he will express his true unconscious, although not what passes with most for the unconscious.

Further, the writer is likely to be a great hand at personal letters, diaries, and autobiographies: indeed, almost the only good autobiographies are those of writers. The writer is more aware of what happens to him or goes on in him and often finds it necessary or useful to be articulate about his inner states, and prides himself on telling the truth. Thus, only a man as devoted to the truth of the emotions as Henry James was would have informed the world, despite his characteristic reticence, of an accident so intimate as his. We must not of course suppose that a writer's statements about his intimate life are equivalent to true statements about his unconscious, which, by definition, he doesn't consciously know; but they may be useful clues to the nature of an entity about which we can make statements of more or less cogency, although never statements of certainty; or they at least give us what is surely related to a knowledge of his unconscious—that is, an insight into his personality.[3]

But while the validity of dealing with the writer's intellectual life in psychoanalytical terms is taken for granted, the psychoanalytical explanation of the intellectual life of scientists is generally speaking not countenanced. The old myth of the mad scientist, with the exception of an occasional mad psychiatrist, no longer exists. The social position of science requires that it should cease, which leads us to remark that those partisans of art who insist on explaining artistic genius by means of psychic imbalance are in effect capitulating to the dominant mores which hold that the members of the respectable professions are, however dull they may be, free from neurosis. Scientists, to continue with them as the best example of the respectable professions, do not usually give us the clues to their personalities which writers habitually give. But no one who has ever lived observantly among scientists will claim that they are without an unconscious or even that they are free from neurosis. How often, indeed, it is apparent that the devotion to science, if it cannot be called a neurotic manifestation, at least can be understood as going very cozily with neurotic elements in the temperament, such as, for example, a marked compulsiveness. Of scientists as a group we can say that they are less concerned with the manifestations of personality, their own or others', than are writers as a group. But this relative indifference is scarcely a sign of normality—indeed, if we choose

---

3. I am by no means in agreement with the statements of Dr. Edmund Bergler about "the" psychology of the writer, but I think that Dr. Bergler has done good service in warning us against taking at their face value a writer's statements about himself, the more especially when they are "frank." Thus, to take Dr. Bergler's notable example, it is usual for biographers to accept Stendhal's statements about his open sexual feelings for his mother when he was a little boy, feelings which went with an intense hatred of his father. But Dr. Bergler believes that Stendhal unconsciously used his consciousness of his love of his mother and of his hatred of his father to mask an unconscious love of his father, which frightened him. ("Psychoanalysis of Writers and of Literary Productivity" in *Psychoanalysis and the Social Sciences*, vol. 1.)

to regard it with the same sort of eye with which the characteristics of writers are regarded, we might say the indifference to
matters of personality is in itself a suspicious evasion.

It is the basic assumption of psychoanalysis that the acts of
every person are influenced by the forces of the unconscious.
Scientists, bankers, lawyers, or surgeons, by reason of the tradi-
tions of their professions, practice concealment and conformity;
but it is difficult to believe that an investigation according to
psychoanalytical principles would fail to show that the strains
and imbalances of their psyches are not of the same frequency as
those of writers, and of similar kind. I do not mean that everybody has the same troubles and identical psyches, but only that
there is no special category for writers.[4]

If this is so, and if we still want to relate the writer's power to
his neurosis, we must be willing to relate all intellectual power
to neurosis. We must find the roots of Newton's power in his
emotional extravagances, and the roots of Darwin's power in his
sorely neurotic temperament, and the roots of Pascal's mathematical genius in the impulses which drove him to extreme
religious masochism—I choose but the classic examples. If we
make the neurosis-power equivalence at all, we must make it in
every field of endeavor. Logician, economist, botanist, physicist,
theologian—no profession may be so respectable or so remote or
so rational as to be exempt from the psychological interpretation.[5]

4. Dr. Bergler believes that there is a particular neurosis of writers, based on
an oral masochism which makes them the enemy of the respectable world,
courting poverty and persecution. But a later development of Dr. Bergler's
theory of oral masochism makes it *the* basic neurosis, not only of writers but
of everyone who is neurotic.

5. In his interesting essay, "Writers and Madness" (*Partisan Review*, January–February 1947), William Barrett has taken issue with this point and has
insisted that a clear distinction is to be made between the relation that exists
between the scientist and his work and the relation that exists between the
artist and his work. The difference, as I understand it, is in the claims of the
ego. The artist's ego makes a claim upon the world which is personal in a way
that the scientist's is not, for the scientist, although he does indeed want prestige and thus "responds to one of the deepest urges of his ego, it is only that
his prestige may come to attend his person through the public world of other
men; and it is not in the end his own being that is exhibited or his own voice
that is heard in the learned report to the Academy." Actually, however, as
is suggested by the sense which mathematicians have of the *style* of mathematical thought, the creation of the abstract thinker is as deeply involved as

Further, not only power but also failure or limitation must be accounted for by the theory of neurosis, and not merely failure or limitation in life but even failure or limitation in art. Thus it is often said that the warp of Dostoevski's mind accounts for the brilliance of his psychological insights. But it is never said that the same warp of Dostoevski's mind also accounted for his deficiency in insight. Freud, who greatly admired Dostoevski, although he did not like him, observed that "his insight was entirely restricted to the workings of the abnormal psyche. Consider his astounding helplessness before the phenomenon of love; he really only understands either crude, instinctive desire or masochistic submission or love from pity."[6] This, we must note, is not merely Freud's comment on the extent of the province which Dostoevski chose for his own, but on his failure to understand what, given the province of his choice, he might be expected to understand.

And since neurosis can account not only for intellectual success and for failure or limitation but also for mediocrity, we have most of society involved in neurosis. To this I have no objection—I think most of society is indeed involved in neurosis. But with

---

the artist's—see *An Essay on the Psychology of Invention in the Mathematical Field* by Jacques Hadamard, Princeton University Press, 1945—and he quite as much as the artist seeks to impose *himself,* to *express* himself. I am of course not maintaining that the processes of scientific thought are the same as those of artistic thought, or even that the scientist's creation is involved with his total personality *in the same way* that the artist's is—I am maintaining only that the scientist's creation is as *deeply* implicated with his total personality as the artist's.

This point of view seems to be supported by Freud's monograph on Leonardo. One of the problems that Freud sets himself is to discover why an artist of the highest endowment should have devoted himself more and more to scientific investigation, with the result that he was unable to complete his artistic enterprises. The particular reasons for this that Freud assigns need not be gone into here; all that I wish to suggest is that Freud understands these reasons to be the working out of an inner conflict, the attempt to deal with the difficulties that have their roots in the most primitive situations. Leonardo's scientific investigations were as necessary and "compelled" and they constituted as much of a claim on the whole personality as anything the artist undertakes; and so far from being carried out for the sake of public prestige, they were largely private and personal, and were thought by the public of his time to be something very like insanity.

6. From a letter quoted in Theodor Reik's *From Thirty Years with Freud* [New York: Farrar & Rinehart, 1940], p. 175.

neurosis accounting for so much, it cannot be made exclusively to account for one man's literary power.

We have now to consider what is meant by genius when its source is identified as the sacrifice and pain of neurosis.

In the case of Henry James, the reference to the neurosis of his personal life does indeed tell us something about the latent intention of his work and thus about the reason for some large part of its interest for us. But if genius and its source are what we are dealing with, we must observe that the reference to neurosis tells us nothing about James's passion, energy, and devotion, nothing about his architectonic skill, nothing about the other themes that were important to him which are not connected with his unconscious concern with castration. We cannot, that is, make the writer's inner life exactly equivalent to his power of expressing it. Let us grant for the sake of argument that the literary genius, as distinguished from other men, is the victim of a "mutilation" and that his fantasies are neurotic.[7] It does not then follow as the inevitable next step that his ability to express these fantasies and to impress us with them is neurotic, for that ability is what we mean by his genius. Anyone might be injured as Henry James was, and even respond within himself to the injury as James is said to have done, and yet not have his literary power.

The reference to the artist's neurosis tells us something about the material on which the artist exercises his powers, and even something about his reasons for bringing his powers into play, but it does not tell us anything about the source of his power, it makes no causal connection between them and the neurosis. And if we look into the matter, we see that there is in fact no causal connection between them. For, still granting that the poet is uniquely neurotic, what is surely not neurotic, what indeed suggests nothing but health, is his power of using his neuroticism. He shapes his fantasies, he gives them social form and reference. Charles Lamb's way of putting this cannot be improved. Lamb

---

7. I am using the word *fantasy*, unless modified, in a neutral sense. A fantasy, in this sense, may be distinguished from the representation of something that actually exists, but it is not opposed to "reality" and not an "escape" from reality. Thus the idea of a rational society, or the image of a good house to be built, as well as the story of something that could never really happen, is a fantasy. There may be neurotic or non-neurotic fantasies.

is denying that genius is allied to insanity; for "insanity" the
modern reader may substitute "neurosis." "The ground of the
mistake," he says,

> is, that men, finding in the raptures of the higher poetry a con-
> dition of exaltation, to which they have no parallel in their own
> experience, besides the spurious resemblance of it in dreams and
> fevers, impute a state of dreaminess and fever to the poet. But the
> true poet dreams being awake. He is not possessed by his subject
> but has dominion over it. . . . Where he seems most to recede from
> humanity, he will be found the truest to it. From beyond the scope
> of nature if he summon possible existences, he subjugates them to
> the law of her consistency. He is beautifully loyal to that sovereign
> directress, when he appears most to betray and desert her. . . . Here-
> in the great and the little wits are differenced; that if the latter
> wander ever so little from nature or natural existence, they lose
> themselves and their readers. . . . They do not create, which implies
> shaping and consistency. Their imaginations are not active— for
> to be active is to call something into act and form—but passive as
> men in sick dreams.

The activity of the artist, we must remember, may be approxi-
mated by many who are themselves not artists. Thus, the expressions of many schizophrenic people have the intense appearance
of creativity and an inescapable interest and significance. But
they are not works of art, and although Van Gogh may have been
schizophrenic he was in addition an artist. Again, as I have already
suggested, it is not uncommon in our society for certain kinds
of neurotic people to imitate the artist in his life and even in his
ideals and ambitions. They follow the artist in everything except
successful performance. It was, I think, Otto Rank who called
such people half-artists and confirmed the diagnosis of their
neuroticism at the same time that he differentiated them from
true artists.

Nothing is so characteristic of the artist as his power of shaping his work, of subjugating his raw material, however aberrant
it be from what we call normality, to the consistency of nature.
It would be impossible to deny that whatever disease or mutilation the artist may suffer is an element of his production which
has its effect on every part of it, but disease and mutilation are
available to us all—life provides them with prodigal generosity.

What marks the artist is his power to shape the material of pain we all have.

At this point, with our recognition of life's abundant provision of pain, we are at the very heart of our matter, which is the meaning we may assign to neurosis and the relation we are to suppose it to have with normality. Here Freud himself can be of help, although it must be admitted that what he tells us may at first seem somewhat contradictory and confusing.

Freud's study of Leonardo da Vinci is an attempt to understand why Leonardo was unable to pursue his artistic enterprises, feeling compelled instead to advance his scientific investigations. The cause of this Freud traces back to certain childhood experiences not different in kind from the experiences which Dr. Rosenzweig adduces to account for certain elements in the work of Henry James. And when he has completed his study Freud makes this *caveat:*

> Let us expressly emphasize that we have never considered Leonardo as a neurotic. . . . We no longer believe that health and disease, normal and nervous, are sharply distinguished from each other. We know today that neurotic symptoms are substitutive formations for certain repressive acts which must result in the course of our development from the child to the cultural man, that we all produce such substitutive formations, and that only the amount, intensity, and distribution of these substitutive formations justify the practical conception of illness. . . .

The statement becomes the more striking when we remember that in the course of his study Freud has had occasion to observe that Leonardo was both homosexual and sexually inactive. I am not sure that the statement that Leonardo was not a neurotic is one that Freud would have made at every point in the later development of psychoanalysis, yet it is in conformity with his continuing notion of the genesis of culture. And the *practical*, the quantitative or economic, conception of illness he insists on in a passage in the *Introductory Lectures*. "The neurotic symptoms," he says,

> . . . are activities which are detrimental, or at least useless, to life as a whole; the person concerned frequently complains of them as obnoxious to him or they involve suffering and distress for him.

The principal injury they inflict lies in the expense of energy they entail, and, besides this, in the energy needed to combat them. Where the symptoms are extensively developed, these two kinds of effort may exact such a price that the person suffers a very serious impoverishment in available mental energy which consequently disables him from all the important tasks of life. This result depends principally upon the amount of energy taken up in this way; therefore you will see that "illness" is essentially a practical conception. But if you look at the matter from a theoretical point of view and ignore this question of degree, you can very well see that we are all ill, i.e., neurotic; for the conditions required for symptom-formation are demonstrable also in normal persons.

We are all ill: the statement is grandiose, and its implications —the implications, that is, of understanding the totality of human nature in the terms of disease—are vast. These implications have never been properly met (although I believe that a few theologians have responded to them), but this is not the place to attempt to meet them. I have brought forward Freud's statement of the essential sickness of the psyche only because it stands as the refutation of what is implied by the literary use of the theory of neurosis to account for genius. For if we are all ill, and if, as I have said, neurosis can account for everything, for failure and mediocrity—"a very serious impoverishment of available mental energy"—as well as for genius, it cannot uniquely account for genius.

This, however, is not to say that there is no connection between neurosis and genius, which would be tantamount, as we see, to saying that there is no connection between human nature and genius. But the connection lies wholly in a particular and special relation which the artist has to neurosis.

In order to understand what this particular and special connection is we must have clearly in mind what neurosis is. The current literary conception of neurosis as a *wound* is quite misleading. It inevitably suggests passivity, whereas, if we follow Freud, we must understand a neurosis to be an *activity*, an activity with a purpose, and a particular kind of activity, a *conflict*. This is not to say that there are no abnormal mental states which are not conflicts. There are; the struggle between elements of the unconscious may never be instituted in the first place, or

it may be called off. As Freud says in a passage which follows
close upon the one I last quoted, "If regressions do not call forth
a prohibition on the part of the ego, no neurosis results; the
libido succeeds in obtaining a real, although not a normal, satisfaction. But if the ego . . . is not in agreement with these regressions, conflict ensues." And in his essay on Dostoevski Freud says
that "there are no neurotic complete masochists," by which he
means that the ego which gives way completely to masochism (or
to any other pathological excess) has passed beyond neurosis;
the conflict has ceased, but at the cost of the defeat of the ego,
and now some other name than that of neurosis must be given
to the condition of the person who thus takes himself beyond the
pain of the neurotic conflict. To understand this is to become
aware of the curious complacency with which literary men regard
mental disease. The psyche of the neurotic is not equally com-
placent; it regards with the greatest fear the chaotic and destructive forces it contains, and it struggles fiercely to keep them at
bay.[8]

We come then to a remarkable paradox: we are all ill, but we
are ill in the service of health, or ill in the service of life, or, at
the very least, ill in the service of life-in-culture. The form of the
mind's dynamics is that of the neurosis, which is to be understood
as the ego's struggle against being overcome by the forces with
which it coexists, and the strategy of this conflict requires that
the ego shall incur pain and make sacrifices of itself, at the same
time seeing to it that its pain and sacrifice be as small as they may.

8. In the article to which I refer in note 5, William Barrett says that he
prefers the old-fashioned term "madness" to "neurosis." But it is not quite
for him to choose—the words do not differ in fashion but in meaning. Most
literary people, when they speak of mental illness, refer to neurosis. Perhaps
one reason for this is that the neurosis is the most benign of the mental ills.
Another reason is surely that psychoanalytical literature deals chiefly with the
neurosis, and its symptomatology and therapy have become familiar; psychoanalysis has far less to say about psychosis, for which it can offer far less
therapeutic hope. Further, the neurosis is easily put into a casual connection
with the social maladjustments of our time. Other forms of mental illness of
a more severe and degenerative kind are not so widely recognized by the literary person and are often assimilated to neurosis with a resulting confusion.
In the present essay I deal only with the conception of neurosis, but this
should not be taken to imply that I believe that other pathological mental
conditions, including actual madness, do not have relevance to the general
matter of the discussion.

But this is characteristic of all minds; no mind is exempt except those which refuse the conflict or withdraw from it; and we ask wherein the mind of the artist is unique. If he is not unique in neurosis, is he then unique in the significance and intensity of his neurosis? I do not believe that we shall go more than a little way toward a definition of artistic genius by answering this question affirmatively. A neurotic conflict cannot ever be either meaningless or merely personal; it must be understood as exemplifying cultural forces of great moment, and this is true of any neurotic conflict at all. To be sure, some neuroses may be more interesting than others, pehaps because they are fiercer or more inclusive; and no doubt the writer who makes a claim upon our interest is a man who by reason of the energy and significance of the forces in struggle within him provides us with the largest representation of the culture in which we, with him, are involved; his neurosis may thus be thought of as having a connection of concomitance with his literary powers. As Freud says in the Dostoevski essay, "the neurosis . . . comes into being all the more readily the richer the complexity which has to be controlled by his ego." Yet even the rich complexity which his ego is doomed to control is not the definition of the artist's genius, for we can by no means say that the artist is preeminent in the rich complexity of elements in conflict within him. The slightest acquaintance with the clinical literature of psychoanalysis will suggest that a rich complexity of struggling elements is no uncommon possession. And that same literature will also make it abundantly clear that the devices of art—the most extreme devices of poetry, for example—are not particular to the mind of the artist but are characteristic of mind itself.

But the artist is indeed unique in one respect, in the respect of his relation to his neurosis. He is what he is by virtue of his successful objectification of his neurosis, by his shaping it and making it available to others in a way which has its effect upon their own egos in struggle. His genius, that is, may be defined in terms of his faculties of perception, representation, and realization, and in these terms alone. It can no more be defined in terms of neurosis than can his power of walking and talking, or his sexuality. The use to which he puts his power, or the manner and style of his power, may be discussed with reference to his particular neurosis, and so may such matters as the untimely diminution or cessation of its exercise. But its essence is irreducible. It is, as we say, a gift.

We are all ill: but even a universal sickness implies an idea of health. Of the artist we must say that whatever elements of neurosis he has in common with his fellow mortals, the one part of him that is healthy, by any conceivable definition of health, is that which gives him the power to conceive, to plan, to work, and to bring his work to a conclusion. And if we are all ill, we are ill by a universal accident, not by a universal necessity, by a fault in the economy of our powers, not by the nature of the powers themselves. The Philoctetes myth, when it is used to imply a causal connection between the fantasy of castration and artistic power, tells us no more about the source of artistic power than we learn about the source of sexuality when the fantasy of castration is adduced, for the fear of castration may explain why a man is moved to extravagant exploits of sexuality, but we do not say that his sexual power itself derives from his fear of castration; and further the same fantasy may also explain impotence or homosexuality. The Philoctetes story, which has so established itself among us as explaining the source of the artist's power, is not really an explanatory myth at all; it is a moral myth having reference to our proper behavior in the circumstances of the universal accident. In its juxtaposition of the wound and the bow, it tells us that we must be aware that weakness does not preclude strength, nor strength weakness. It is therefore not irrelevant to the artist, but when we use it we will do well to keep in mind the other myths of the arts, recalling what Pan and Dionysius suggest of the relation of art to physiology and superabundance, remembering that to Apollo were attributed the bow and the lyre, two strengths together, and that he was given the lyre by its inventor, the baby Hermes—that miraculous infant who, the day he was born, left his cradle to do mischief: and the first thing he met with was a tortoise, which he greeted politely before scooping it from its shell, and, thought and deed being one with him, he contrived the instrument to which he sang "the glorious tale of his own begetting." These were gods, and very early ones, but their myths tell us something about the nature and source of art even in our grim, late human present.

Susan Sontag

———•———

Marat/Sade/Artaud

Earlier we followed one critic, Eric Bentley, on an excursion into the world of therapy. Here Susan Sontag considers some of the same ideas, but stays within the framework of theatrical drama—specifically, Peter Weiss's Marat/Sade, *a play within a play within a psychiatric institution.*

> The Primary and most beautiful of Nature's qualities is motion, which agitates her at all times. But this motion is simply the perpetual consequence of crimes; and it is conserved by means of crimes alone.
>
> —SADE

> Everything that acts is a cruelty. It is upon this idea of extreme action, pushed beyond all limits, that theatre must be rebuilt.
>
> —ARTAUD

Theatricality and insanity—the two most potent subjects of the contemporary theater—are brilliantly fused in Peter Weiss' play, *The Persecution and Assassination of Marat as Performed by the Inmates of the Asylum at Charenton under the Direction of the Marquis de Sade*. The subject is a dramatic performance staged before the audience's eyes; the scene is a madhouse. The historical facts behind the play are that in the insane asylum just outside Paris where Sade was confined by order of Napoleon for the last

SOURCE: Reprinted with the permission of Farrar, Straus & Giroux, Inc. from *Against Interpretation* by Susan Sontag, Copyright © 1961, 1962, 1963, 1964, 1965, 1966 by Susan Sontag.

eleven years of his life (1803–14), it was the enlightened policy of the director, M. Coulmier, to allow Charenton's inmates to stage theatrical productions of their own devising which were open to the Parisian public. In these circumstances Sade is known to have written and put on several plays (all lost), and Weiss' play ostensibly re-creates such a performance. The year is 1808, and the stage is the stark tiled bathhouse of the asylum.

Theatricality permeates Weiss' cunning play in a peculiarly modern sense: most of *Marat/Sade* consists of a play-within-a-play. In Peter Brook's production, which opened in London last August, the aged, disheveled, flabby Sade (acted by Patrick Magee) sits quietly on the left side of the stage—prompting (with the aid of a fellow-patient who acts as stage manager and narrator), supervising, commenting. M. Coulmier, dressed formally and wearing some sort of honorific red sash, attended by his elegantly dressed wife and daughter, sits throughout the performance on the right side of the stage. There is also an abundance of theatricality in a more traditional sense: the emphatic appeal to the senses with spectacle and sound. A quartet of inmates with string hair and painted faces, wearing colored sacks and floppy hats, sing sardonic loony songs while the action described by the songs is mimed; their motley getup contrasts with the shapeless white tunics and strait-jackets, the whey-colored faces of most of the rest of the inmates who act in Sade's passion play on the French Revolution. The verbal action, conducted by Sade, is repeatedly interrupted by brilliant bits of acting-out performed by the lunatics, the most forceful of which is a mass guillotining sequence, in which some inmates make metallic rasping noises, bang together parts of the ingenious set, and pour buckets of paint (blood) down drains, while other madmen gleefully jump into a pit in the center of the stage, leaving their heads piled above stage level, next to the guillotine.

In Brook's production, insanity proves the most authoritative and sensuous kind of theatricality. Insanity establishes the inflection, the intensity of *Marat/Sade,* from the opening image of the ghostly inmates who are to act in Sade's play, crouching in foetal postures or in a catatonic stupor or trembling or performing some obsessive ritual, then stumbling forward to greet the affable M. Coulmier and his family as they enter the stage and mount the platform where they will sit. Insanity is the register of the intensity of the individual performances as well: of Sade, who recites his long speeches with a painful clenched singsong deliberateness; of Marat (acted by Clive Revill), swathed in wet clothes (a treatment for his skin disease) and encased throughout the action in a portable metal bathtub, even in the midst of the most passionate declamation staring straight ahead as though he were already dead; of Charlotte Corday, Marat's assassin, who is played by a beautiful somnambule who periodically goes blank, forgets her lines, even lies down on the stage and has to be awakened by Sade; of Duperret, the Girondist deputy and lover of Corday, played by a lanky stiff-haired patient, an erotomaniac, who is constantly breaking down in his role of gentleman and lover and lunging lustfully toward the patient playing Corday (in the course of the play, he has to be put in a strait-jacket); of Simone Everard, Marat's mistress and nurse, played by an almost wholly disabled patient who can barely speak and is limited to jerky idiot movements as she changes Marat's dressings. Insanity becomes the privileged, most authentic metaphor for passion; or, what's the same thing in this case, the logical terminus of any strong emotion. Both dream (as in the "Marat's Nightmare" sequence) and dreamlike states must end in violence. Being "calm" amounts to a failure to understand one's real situation. Thus, the slow-motion staging of Corday's murder of Marat (history, i.e., theater) is followed by the inmates shouting and singing of the fifteen bloody years since then, and ends with the "cast" assaulting the Coulmiers as they attempt to leave the stage.

It is through its depiction of theatricality and insanity that Weiss' play is also a play of ideas. The heart of the play is a running debate between Sade, in his chair, and Marat, in his bath, on the meaning of the French Revolution, that is, on the psychological and political premises of modern history, but seen through a very modern sensibility, one equipped with the hindsight afforded by the Nazi concentration camps. But Marat/Sade does not lend itself to being formulated as a particular theory about modern experience. Weiss' play seems to be more about the range of sensibility that concerns itself with, or is at stake in, the modern experience, than it is about an argument or an interpretation of that experience. Weiss does not present ideas as much as he immerses his audience in them. Intellectual debate is the material of the play, but it is not its subject or its end. The Charenton setting ensures that this debate takes place in a constant atmosphere of barely suppressed violence: all ideas are volatile at this temperature. Again, insanity proves to be the most austere (even abstract) and drastic mode of expressing in theatrical terms the reenacting of ideas, as members of the cast reliving the Revolution run amuck and have to be restrained and the cries of the Parisian mob for liberty are suddenly metamorphosed into the cries of the patients howling to be let out of the asylum.

Such theater, whose fundamental action is the irrevocable careening toward extreme states of feeling, can end in only two ways. It can turn in on itself and become formal, and end in strict *da capo* fashion, with its own opening lines. Or it can turn outward, breaking the "frame," and assault the audience. Ionesco has admitted that he orginally envisaged his first play, *The Bald Soprano,* ending with a massacre of the audience; in another version of the same play (which now ends *da capo*), the author was to leap on the stage, and shout imprecations at the audience till they fled the theater. Brook, or Weiss, or both, have devised for the end of *Marat/Sade* an equivalent of the same hostile gesture toward the audience. The inmates, that is, the "cast" of Sade's play, have gone berserk and assaulted the Coulmiers; but this riot—that is, the play—is broken off by the entry of the stage manager of the Aldwych Theater, in modern skirt, sweater, and gym shoes. She blows a whistle; the actors abruptly stop, turn, and face the audience; but when the audience applauds, the company responds with a slow ominous handclap, drowning out the "free" applause and leaving everyone pretty uncomfortable.

My own admiration for, and pleasure in, *Marat/Sade* is virtually unqualified. The play that opened in London last August, and will, it's rumored, soon be seen in New York, is one of the great experiences of anyone's theater-going lifetime. Yet almost everyone, from the daily reviewers to the most serious critics, has voiced serious reservations about, if not outright dislike for, Brook's production of Weiss' play. Why?

Three ready-made ideas seem to me to underlie most caviling at Weiss' play in Brook's production of it.

The Connection between Theater and Literature. One ready-made idea: a work of theater is a branch of literature. The truth is, some works of theater may be judged primarily as works of literature, others not.

It is because this is not admitted, or generally understood, that one reads all too frequently the statement that while *Marat/Sade* is, theatrically, one of the most stunning things anyone has seen on the stage, it's a "director's play," meaning a first-rate production of a second-rate play. A well-known English poet told me he detested the play for this reason: because although he thought it marvelous when he saw it, he *knew* that if it hadn't had the benefit of Peter Brook's production, he wouldn't have liked it. It's also reported that the play in Konrad Swinarski's production last year in West Berlin made nowhere near the striking impression it does in the current production in London.

Granted, *Marat/Sade* is not the supreme masterpiece of contemporary dramatic literature, but it is scarcely a second-rate play. Considered as a text alone, *Marat/Sade* is both sound and exciting. It is not the play which is at fault, but a narrow vision of theater which insists on one image of the director—as servant to the writer, bringing out meanings already resident in the text.

After all, to the extent that it is true that Weiss' text, in Adrian Mitchell's graceful translation, is enhanced greatly by being joined with Peter Brook's staging, what of it? Apart from a theater of dialogue (of language) in which the text is primary, there is also a theater of the senses. The first might be called "play," the second "theater work." In the case of a pure theater work, the writer who sets down words which are to be spoken by actors and staged by a director loses his primacy. In this case, the "author" or "creator" is, to quote Artaud, none other than "the person who controls the direct handling of the stage." The director's art is a material art—an art in which he deals with the bodies of actors, props, the lights, the music. And what Brook has put together is particularly brilliant and inventive—the rhythm of the staging, the costumes, the ensemble mime scenes. In every detail of the production—one of the most remarkable elements of which is the clangorous tuneful music (by Richard Peaslee) featuring bells, cymbals, and the organ—there is an inexhaustible material inventiveness, a relentless address to the senses. Yet, something about Brook's sheer virtuosity in stage effects offends. It seems, to most people, to overwhelm the text. But perhaps that's just the point.

I'm not suggesting that *Marat/Sade* is simply theater of the senses. Weiss has supplied a complex and highly literate text which demands to be responded to. But *Marat/Sade* also demands to be taken on the sensory level as well, and only the sheerest prejudice about what theater must be (the prejudice, namely, that a work of theater is to be judged, in the last analysis, as a branch of literature) lies behind the demand that the written, and subsequently spoken, text of a theater work carry the whole play.

The Connection between Theater and Psychology. Another ready-made idea: drama consists of the revelation of character, built on the conflict of realistically credible motives. But the most interesting modern theater is a theater which goes beyond psychology.

Again, to cite Artaud: "We need true action, but without practical consequences. It is not on the social level that the action of theater unfolds. Still less on the ethical and psychological levels. . . . This obstinacy in making characters talk about feelings, passions, desires, and impulses of a strictly psychological order, in which a single word is to compensate for innumerable gestures, is the reason . . . the theater has lost its true *raison d'être.*"

It's from this point of view, tendentiously formulated by Artaud, that one may properly approach the fact that Weiss has situated his argument in an insane asylum. The fact is that with the exception of the audience-figures on stage—M. Coulmier, who frequently interrupts the performance to remonstrate with Sade, and his wife and daughter, who have no lines—all the characters in the play are mad. But the setting of *Marat/Sade* does not amount to a statement that the world is insane. Nor is it an instance of a fashionable interest in the psychology of psychopathic behavior. On the contrary, the concern with insanity in art today usually reflects the desire to go beyond psychology. By representing characters with deranged behavior or deranged styles of speech, such dramatists as Pirandello, Genet, Beckett, and Ionesco make it unnecessary for their characters to embody in their acts or voice in their speech sequential and credible accounts of their motives. Freed from the limitations of what Artaud calls "psychological and dialogue painting of the individual," the dramatic representation is open to levels of experience which are more heroic, more rich in fantasy, more philosophical. The point applies, of course, not only to the drama. The choice of "insane" behavior as the subject-matter of art is, by now, the virtually classic strategy of modern artists who wish to transcend traditional "realism," that is, psychology.

Take the scene to which many people particularly objected, in which Sade persuades Charlotte Corday to whip him (Peter Brook has her do it with her hair)—while he, meanwhile, continues to recite, in agonized tones, some point about the Revolution, and the nature of human nature. The purpose of this scene is surely not to inform the audience that, as one critic put it, Sade is "sick, sick, sick"; nor is it fair to reproach Weiss' Sade, as the same critic does, with "using the theater less to advance an argument than to excite himself." (Anyway, why not both?) By combining rational or near-rational argument with irrational behavior, Weiss is not inviting the audience to make a judgment on Sade's character, mental competence, or state of mind. Rather, he is shifting to a kind of theater focused not on characters, but on intense transpersonal emotions borne by characters. He is providing a kind of vicarious emotional experience (in this case, frankly erotic) from which the theater has shied away too long.

Language is used in *Marat/Sade* primarily as a form of incantation, instead of being limited to the revelation of character and the exchange of ideas. This use of language as incantation is the point of another scene which many who saw the play have found objectionable, upsetting, and gratuitous—the bravura soliloquy of Sade, in which he illustrates the cruelty in the heart of man by relating in excruciating detail the public execution by slow dismemberment of Damiens, the would-be assassin of Louis XV.

The Connection between Theater and Ideas. Another ready-made idea: a work of art is to be understood as being "about" or representing or arguing for an "idea." That being so, an implicit standard for a work of art is the value of the ideas it contains, and whether these are clearly and consistently expressed.

It is only to be expected that *Marat/Sade* would be subjected to these standards. Weiss' play, theatrical to its core, is also full of intelligence. It contains discussions of the deepest issues of contemporary morality and history and feeling that put to shame the banalities peddled by such would-be diagnosticans of these issues as Arthur Miller (see his current *After the Fall* and *Incident at Vichy*), Friedrich Duerrenmatt (*The Visit, The Physicists*), and Max Frisch (*Andorra, The Firebugs*). Yet, there is no doubt that *Marat/Sade* is intellectually puzzling. Argument is offered, only (seemingly) to be undermined by the context of the play—the insane asylum, and the avowed theatricality of the proceedings. People do seem to represent positions in Weiss' play. Roughly, Sade represents the claim of the permanence of human nature, in all its vileness, against Marat's revolutionary fervor and his belief that man can be changed by history. Sade thinks that "the world is made of bodies," Marat that it is made of forces. Secondary characters, too, have their moments of passionate advocacy: Duperret hails the eventual dawn of freedom, the priest Jacques Roux denounces Napoleon. But Sade and "Marat" are both madmen, each in a different style; "Charlotte Corday" is a sleepwalker, "Duperret" has satyriasis; "Roux" is hysterically violent. Doesn't this undecut their arguments? And, apart from the question of the context of insanity in which the ideas are presented, there is the device of the play-within-a-play. At one level, the running debate between Sade and Marat, in which the moral and social idealism attributed to Marat is countered by Sade's transmoral advococy of the claims of individual passion, seems a debate between equals. But, on another level, since the fiction of Weiss' play is that it is Sade's script which Marat is reciting, presumably Sade carries the argument. One critic goes so far as to say that because Marat has to double as a puppet in Sade's psychodrama, and as Sade's opponent in an evenly matched ideological contest, the debate between them is stillborn. And, lastly, some critics have attacked the play on the grounds of its lack of historical fidelity to the actual views of Marat, Sade, Duperret, and Roux.

These are some of the difficulties which have led people to charge *Marat/Sade* with being obscure or intellectually shallow. But most of these difficulties, and the objections made to them, are misunderstandings—misunderstandings of the connection between the drama and didacticism. Weiss' play cannot be treated like an argument of Arthur Miller, or even of Brecht. We have to do here with a kind of theater as different from these as Antonioni and Godard are from Eisenstein. Weiss' play contains an argument, or rather it employs the material of intellectual debate and historical reevaluation (the nature of human nature, the betrayal of the Revolution, etc.). But Weiss' play is only secondarily an argument. There is another use of ideas to be reckoned with in art: ideas as sensory stimulants. Antonioni has said of his films that he wants them to dispense with "the superannuated casuistry of positives and negatives." The same impulse discloses itself in a complex way in *Marat/Sade*. Such a position does not mean that these artists wish to dispense with ideas. What it does mean is that ideas, including moral ideas, are proffered in a new style. Ideas may function as décor, props, sensuous material.

One might perhaps compare the Weiss play with the long prose narratives of Genet. Genet is not really arguing that "cruelty is good" or "cruelty is holy" (a moral statement, albeit the opposite of traditional morality), but rather shifting the argument to another plane, from the moral to the aesthetic. But this is not quite the case with *Marat/Sade*. While the "cruelty" in *Marat/Sade* is not, ultimately, a moral issue, it is not an aesthetic one either. It is an ontological issue. While those who propose the aesthetic version of "cruelty" interest themselves in the richness of the surface of life, the proponents of the ontological version of "cruelty" want their art to act out the widest possible context for human action, at least a wider context than that provided by realistic art. That wider context is what Sade calls "nature" and what Artaud means when he says that "everything that acts is a cruelty." There is a moral vision in art like *Marat/Sade*, though clearly it cannot (and this has made its audience uncomfortable) be summed up with the slogans of "humanism." But "humanism" is not identical with morality. Precisely, art like *Marat/Sade* entails a rejection of "humanism," of the task of moralizing the world and thereby refusing to acknowledge the "crimes" of which Sade speaks.

I have repeatedly cited the writings of Artaud on the theater in discussing *Marat/Sade*. But Artaud—unlike Brecht, the other great theoretician of 20th century theater—did not create a body of work to illustrate his theory and sensibility.

Often, the sensibility (the theory, at a certain level of discourse) which governs certain works of art is formulated before there exist substantial works to embody that sensibility. Or, the theory may apply to works other than those for which they are developed. Thus, right now in France writers and critics such as Alain Robbe-Grillet *(Pour un Nouveau Roman)*, Roland Barthes *(Essais Critiques)*, and Michel Foucault (essays in *Tel Quel* and elsewhere) have worked out an elegant and persuasive anti-rhetorical aesthetic for the novel. But the novels produced by the *nouveau roman* writers and analyzed by them are in fact not as important or satisfying an illustration of this sensibility as certain films, and, moreover, films by directors, Italian as well as French, who have no connection with this school of new French writers, such as Bresson, Melville, Antonioni, Godard, and Bertolucci *(Before the Revolution)*.

Similarly, it seems doubtful that the only stage production which Artaud personally supervised, of Shelley's *The Cenci*, or the 1948 radio broadcast *Pour en Finir avec le Jugement de Dieu*, came close to following the brilliant recipes for the theater in his writings, any more than did his public readings of Seneca's tragedies. We have up to now lacked a full-fledged example of Artaud's category, "the theater of cruelty." The closest thing to it are the theatrical events done in New York and elsewhere in the last five years, largely by painters (such as Alan Kaprow, Claes Oldenberg, Jim Dine, Bob Whitman, Red Grooms, Robert Watts) and without text or at least intelligible speech, called Happenings. Another example of work in a quasi-Artaudian spirit: the brilliant staging by Lawrence Kornfield and Al Carmines of Gertrude Stein's prose poem "What Happened," at the Judson Memorial Church last year. Another example: the final production of the Living Theatre in New York, Kenneth H. Brown's *The Brig*, directed by Judith Malina.

All the works I have mentioned so far suffer, though, apart from all questions of individual execution, from smallness of scope and conception—as well as a narrowness of sensory means. Hence, the great interest of *Marat/Sade*, for it, more than any modern theater work I know of, comes near the scope, as well as the intent, of Artaud's theater. (I must reluctantly except, because I have never seen it, what sounds like the most interesting and ambitious theater group in the world today—the Theater Laboratory of Jerzy Grotowski in Opole, Poland. For an account of this work, which is an ambitious extension of Artaudian principles, see the *Tulane Drama Review*, Spring 1965.)

Yet Artaud's is not the only major influence reflected in the Weiss-Brook production. Weiss is reported to have said that in this play he wished—staggering ambition!—to combine Brecht and Artaud. And, to be sure, one can see what he means. Certain features of *Marat/Sade* are reminiscent of Brecht's theater—constructing the action around a debate on principles and reasons; the songs; the appeals to the audience through an M.C. And these blend well with the Artaudian texture of the situation and the staging. Yet the matter is not that simple. Indeed, the final question that Weiss' play raises is precisely the one of the ultimate compatibility of these two sensibilities and ideals. How *could* one reconcile Brecht's conception of a didactic theater, a theater of intelligence, with Artuad's theater of magic, of gesture, of "cruelty," of feeling?

The answer seems to be that, if one could effect such a reconciliation or synthesis, Weiss' play has taken a big step toward doing so. Hence the obtuseness of the critic who complained: "Useless ironies, insoluble conundrums, double meanings which could be multipled indefinitely: Brecht's machinery without Brecht's incisiveness or firm commitment," forgetting about Artaud altogether. If one does put the two together, one sees that new perceptions must be allowed, new standards devised. For isn't an Artaudian theater of commitment, much less "firm commitment," a contradiction in terms? Or is it? The problem is not solved by ignoring the fact that Weiss in *Marat/Sade* means to employ ideas in a fugue form (rather than as literal assertions), and therby necessarily refers beyond the arena of social material and didactic statement. A misunderstanding of the artistic aims implicit in *Marat/Sade* due to a narrow vision of the theater accounts for most of the critics' dissatisfaction with Weiss' play— an ungrateful dissatisfaction, considering the extraordinary richness of the text and of the Brook production. That the ideas taken up in *Marat/Sade* are not resolved, in an intellectual sense, is far less important than the extent to which they do work together in the sensory arena.

Rollo May

·

Creativity and Encounter

Art is frequently understood as something that comes out of someone—which indeed it does, but it comes only as a result of someone's interaction with the world outside the self. Rollo May speaks of art as an encounter, an encounter with a random universe that is made meaningful by the individual's act of creation. And the mental processes that he invokes to describe such creation—"accept the anxiety, confront it, and use it"—could as easily be a description of successful therapy.

In this paper I shall not use our usual psychological language. I am not inclined to apologize for this, since I believe that most of our approaches to creativity in psychology have been strikingly inadequate. Essentially we have come up with what the artists and poets smile at and say, "Interesting, yes. But it has next to nothing to do with what is actually going on within me in the creative act." There have been notable exceptions to this tendency, of course: the works of MacKinnon, Frank Barron, Crutchfield, and Harold Anderson, for example, and the insistence of Allport, Rogers, and Maslow that creativity be studied not merely as an aspect of neurosis, or reductively, but in its own right as a positive aspect of personality. But, in general, we have come up with truisms or irrelevancies.

SOURCE: "Creativity and Encounter" is published as it originally appeared in *The American Journal of Psychoanalysis*, Vol. XXIV, No. 1, 1964. It appears in a revised form in Rollo May's *The Courage to Create*, W. W. Norton & Company, 1975. Reprinted by permission of *The American Journal of Psychoanalysis* and the author.

It is not that I believe that the ideas which I will put forth cannot be phrased in psychological language; I think they can, and also can to some extent be tested and understood by empirical methods. However, I believe our pressing problem at this stage is that we have not grasped the nature of creativity as such.

I wish, therefore, to propose a theory, and make some remarks about it arising largely out of my contacts and discussions with artists and poets themselves. The theory is: *Creativity occurs in an act of encounter, and is to be understood with this encounter as its center.*

Cézanne sees a tree. He sees it in a way no one else has ever seen it. He experiences, as he no doubt would say, a "being grasped" by the tree. The painting that issues out of this encounter between a person, Cézanne, and an objective reality, the tree, is literally new. Something is born, comes into being, something which did not exist before—which is as good a definition of creativity as we can get. Thereafter everyone who has the experience of encounter with the painting, who looks at it with intensity of awareness and lets it speak to him, will see the tree with the unique powerful movement and the architectural beauty which literally did not exist in our relation with trees until Cézanne experienced and painted them.

The very fact that the creative act is such an encounter between two poles is what makes it so hard to study. It is easy enough to find the subjective pole, the person, but it is much harder to define the objective pole, the "world" or "reality." Since my emphasis here is on the encounter itself, I shall not worry too much at the moment about such definitions. Archibald MacLeish, in his book *Poetry and Experience,* uses the most universal terms possible for the two poles of the encounter: being and non-being. He quotes a Chinese poet: "We poets struggle with non-being to force it to yield being. We knock upon silence for an answering music."

MacLeish goes on:

> Consider what this means. The "being" which the poem is to contain derives from "non-being," not from the poet. And the "music" which the poem is to own comes not from us who make the poem but from the silence; comes in *answer* to our knock. The verbs are eloquent: "struggle," "force," "knock." The poet's labor is not to

wait until the cry gathers of itself in his own throat. The poet's labor is to struggle with the meaninglessness and silence of the world until he can force it to mean; until he can make the silence answer and the non-being be. It is a labor which undertakes to "know" the world not by exegesis or demonstration or proofs, but directly, as a man knows apple in his mouth.

One of our most serious errors in psychoanalysis has been the attempt to find something within the individual which is then projected onto the work of art, or something in his early experience which is transferred to the canvas, the poem. Obviously, early experiences play exceedingly important roles in determining how the artist will encounter his world; but this subjective data can never explain the encounter itself. Even in the case of abstract artists, where the process of painting seems most subjective, the encounter is present and may be sparked by the artist's encountering the brilliant colors on his palette or the inviting rough whiteness of his canvas. Mark Tobey fills his canvases with elliptical calligraphic lines, beautiful whirls which seem at first glance to be completely abstract and to come from nowhere at all except his own subjective processes. But I shall never forget how struck I was to see strewn around in Tobey's studio books on astronomy and photographs of the Milky Way. And I knew that Tobey experiences the movement of stars and solar constellations as the external pole to his encounter.

Out of the encounter is born the work of art. W. H. Auden once remarked: "The poet marries the language, and out of this marriage the poem is born." How *active* this makes language in the creating of a poem! It is not at all that language is merely a tool of communication, or that we only use language to express our poem—it is just as true that language uses *us*. Language is the symbolic repository of the meaningful experience of ourselves and our fellow human beings down through history, and, as such, it reaches out to grasp us in the creating of a poem. Thus the original Greek and Hebrew words meaning "to know" meant also "to have sexual relations." One reads in the Bible, "Abraham knew his wife and she conceived." The etymology of the term demonstrates the prototypal fact that knowledge, as well as poetry and other creative products, arises out of the dynamic encounter between subjective and objective poles.

The particular forms these offspring take are "symbols" and "myths." (I do not use *symbols* in the abstract sense of mathematical symbols—these, accurately speaking, are signs, not symbols.) The symbol and myth are the living, immediate forms which emerge from encounter, and they express the interrelationship of subjective and objective poles. Symbols (like Cézanne's tree) or myths (like Oedipus) express the relationship between subject and object, between conscious and unconscious experience, between one's individual present history and human history. They are born out of the heightened consciousness of the encounter we are describing, and they have their power to grasp us because they require from us and give to us an experience of heightened consciousness.[1]

Thus, one distinguishing characteristic of the encounter is some degree of intensity, or what I would call passion. Hans Hofmann, venerable dean of abstract painters in this country and one of our most expert and experienced teachers, remarked that art students these days have a great deal of talent but what they lack is passion, commitment. Hofmann went on to say, interestingly enough, that his men students get married early for reasons of security and become dependent on their wives, and that often it is only through their wives that he can draw out their talent. The fact that talent is plentiful but passion is lacking seems to me to be a very important facet of the problem of creativity in many fields in our day, and our ways of approaching creativity by evading the encounter have played directly into these trends. We worship technique (talent) as a way of evading the anxiety of the direct encounter.

Kierkegaard knew this so well! "The present writer," he wrote about himself, ". . . can easily foresee his fate in an age when passion has been obliterated in favor of learning, in an age when

1. Thus in the history of culture artistic activity precedes other forms. As Sir Herbert Read puts it, "On the basis of this [artistic] activity, a 'symbolic discourse' becomes possible, and religion, philosophy and science follow as consequent modes of thought." This is not to say that art is the more primitive form in a pejorative sense, reason the more civilized—an egregious error unfortunately often found in our rationalistic Western culture. It is, rather, to say that the creative encounter in the art form is "total," expresses a wholeness of experience; and science and philosophy abstract partial aspects for their subsequent study.

an author who wants to have readers must take care to write in such a way that the book can easily be perused during the afternoon nap."

We see at this point the inadequacy of the concept commonly used in psychoanalytic circles to explain creativity: "regression in the service of the ego." In my own endeavors to understand creative people in psychoanalysis and to understand the creative act in general, I have found this theory unsatisfactory not only because of its negative character, but chiefly because it proposes a partial solution which diverts us from the center of the creative act and therefore away from any full understanding of creativity. I grant that creativity often seems to be a regressive phenomenon because it brings out archaic, infantile, unconscious psychic contents. But this is a result rather than a cause, and when these archaic elements have genuine power to move others and a universality of meaning—that is, become genuine symbols—it is because some encounter is occurring on a more basic, comprehensive level.

Ernst Kris, in supporting the theory of "regression in the service of the ego," cites the case of the minor poet A. E. Housman, who, in his autobiography, describes his way of writing poetry as follows: After a full morning of teaching his classes in Latin at Oxford, Housman would have lunch, with which he drank a pint of beer, then take a walk. And in this somnambulistic mood of the walk his poems came to him. Kris, in line with this theory, correlates passiveness and receptivity with creativity. It is true that most of us find an appeal in such lines of Housman as these:

> Be still, my soul, be still,
> The arms you bear are brittle . . .

And the appeal does have a nostalgic, regressive mood.

If, however, we take as contrast some lines from one of the major poets of our day, W. B. Yeats, we find a quite different mood. In his poem, "The Second Coming," Yeats describes modern man's condition:

> Things fall apart; the centre cannot hold;
> Mere anarchy is loosed upon the world. . . .

He then tells us what he sees:

> The Second Coming! Hardly are those words out
> When a vast image . . .
> Troubles my sight; somewhere in sands of the desert
> A shape with lion body and the head of a man,
> A gaze blank and pitiless as the sun,
> Is moving its slow thighs. . . .
> And what rough beast, its hour come round at last,
> Slouches towards Bethlehem to be born?

Our experience of this last symbol is one of tremendous power, revealing in a new way, with beauty but with terrible meaning at the same time, the situation we modern men find ourselves in. The reason Yeats has such power is that he writes out of an intensity of consciousness which includes archaic elements because they are part of him, as of every man, and will emerge in any intensity of awareness. But the symbol has its power precisely from the fact that it is an encounter which also includes the most dedicated and passionate intellectual effort. As MacLeish has told us, "The poet's labor is not to wait until the cry gathers of itself in his own throat."

Obviously, poetic and creative insights of all sorts come to us in moments of relaxation. They come not haphazardly, however, but come only in those areas in which we are intensively committed and upon which we concentrate intensively in our waking, conscious experience. It may be, indeed, that the insights can break through only in moments of relaxation; but this is *how* it comes rather than explaining its genesis. My friends who are poets tell me that if you want to write poetry, or even read it, the hour after a full morning of teaching and a full lunch and a pint of beer is just the time *not* to pick; choose rather the moments in which you are capable of highest, most intense consciousness. If you write poetry during your afternoon nap, it will be perused that way.

The issue here is not simply which poets you happen to like. It is much more basic—namely, the nature of the symbols and myths which are born in the creative act. Symbol and myth do bring into awareness infantile, archaic, unconscious longings, dreads and similar psychic content—this is their regressive aspect. But they also bring out new meaning, new forms, disclose reality which was literally not present before, a reality that is not merely subjective but has a second pole which is outside ourselves—this is the progressive side of symbol and myth. This aspect points ahead: it is integrative; it is a progressive revealing of structure in our relation to nature and our own existence; it is a road to universals beyond discrete concrete personal experience. It is this second, progressive aspect of symbols and myths that is almost completely omitted in the traditional Freudian psychoanalytic approach.

This heightened consciousness which we have identified as characteristic of the encounter, the state in which the dichotomy between subjective experience and objective reality is overcome and symbols which reveal new meaning are born, is historically termed ecstasy.[2] It is highly interesting that in psychology we dodge that problem, Maslow's work on the peak experience being a notable exception. Or when we do study ecstasy we are implicitly pejorative, or assume outright that it is neurotic.

The experience of encounter brings with it anxiety. I do not need here to remind you of all the testimony by artists and creative people of their "fear and trembling" in their moments of creative encounter. They also use the word "joy," or an equivalent, which illustrates the positive aspect of anxiety. The myth of Prometheus is the classical expression of this anxiety. W. H. Auden once remarked, in answer to my question, that he always experiences anxiety in his writing of poetry except when he is "playing." Playing may be defined as encounter in which anxiety is temporarily postponed.

According to the theory proposed in this paper, anxiety is an understandable concomitant of the shaking of the self-world relationship which occurs in the encounter. Our self-system and sense of identity are literally shaken; the world is not as we experienced it before, and since self and world are always correlated, we no longer are what we were before. Past, present, and future

2. I do not, of course, mean ecstasy in the popular sense of hysterical. Like passion, ecstasy is a quality of emotion (or more accurately, a quality of relationship one side of which is emotional) rather than quantity. Ecstasy is *ex-stasis*, a temporary transcending of the subject-object dichotomy.

form a new gestalt. Obviously this is only rarely true in a complete sense (Gaugin going to the South Sea Islands, or Van Gogh becoming psychotic), but it is literally true that the creative encounter does change to some degree the world-self relationship. The anxiety we feel is temporary rootlessness, disorientation; it is the anxiety of nothingness.

This is why I have been so impressed by Frank Barron's studies of creative persons. Presenting cards, some with orderly and symmetrical designs, and others, disorderly and irregular, he found that the average person liked and chose the orderly, symmetrical cards. But the creative persons, both scientists and artists, much more frequently chose the disorderly cards. They chose the "broken" universe; they got joy out of encountering it and forming it into order. They could accept the anxiety, confront it, and use it in molding their disorderly universe "closer to the heart's desire."

The creative person, as I see him, is characterized by the fact that he can live with this anxiety, even though he may pay a high price in terms of insecurity, sensitivity, and defenselessness for his gift of the "divine madness," as the Greeks called it. He does not run away from non-being, as MacLeish tells us, but by encountering and wrestling with non-being, he forces it to produce being. He knocks upon silence and meaninglessness until he can force it to mean.

David Ahlstrom

The Suicide of Art

Art is a creation, and it is also—sometimes subtly, sometimes outrageously—destruction. Artaud talked about people in a play attacking the audience; David Ahlstrom, a teacher of art, here speaks with equal approval of artists smashing violins. Such ideas may seem to be utterly irrational—mad, crazy, insane—but yet they contain a wise awareness of the truth that creation, whether you call it therapy or art or evolution, is change; that when something new is born, something old dies; and that death is often violent.

Why is it that artists do such strange things? Why do they smash pianos, burn violins? Why is it that artists talk of destroying art, of burning the museums, of lynching college professors? Are these ideas just silly things that are said without complete seriousness? Are they said to make good reading later on? Are they the rantings of "characters," of colorful "artist types"? Hardly! They are the most serious, solemn (ludicrous, comical) early warnings of the men who live, those who live with their own lives the contradictions in our selves and in our society (not that we do not live the same contradictions, but while the rest of us tend to ignore, repress, forget them, the artists always remain at least partly conscious of them, and hence explicitly seek to change themselves, us, our-their society, in an attempt to resolve them). These artists warn us that what we see is not what they see, that

SOURCE: This piece, which appeared in Volume 8, Number 1, of *Arts in Society*, is being published with the permission of the editors.

quite likely we are blind; that what we seem to feel is not what they feel, that we are actually, in all likelihood, unfeeling. We ignore them at our own peril.

Everyone seems to be able to agree that art is some kind of communication. What does wholly destructive art communicate? Well, it seems to me that communication between the members of groups of people, whether these be collections of artists concerned with their art and their society, or citizens concerned with political matters or specific supposed rights, may communicate with their established institutions, their leaders, their contemporaries, in just four ways: They can make verbal or written statements, hopefully bringing about dialogue and perhaps change. Failing this, and given a bit of wit, they may resort to public satire on an artistic or on another level. Failing here, they may attempt a peaceful, non-violent demonstration. With still no results, the remaining step is violence.

Perhaps it may be generally agreed that the placing of political matters and matters of war and peace alongside artistic matters, as I have done here, is not an idle or capricious gesture. One matter is as deadly earnest as the other. For, as I have intimated, artists know things that other members of the society seem not to understand. If they are ignored, as has almost universally been the case, the results can and will be wholly unnecessary anguish if not utter catastrophe.

We live in a society of institutions, each one set up to fight the last war all over again; to subsidize art that had relevance only to our great-grandfathers; to govern cities of blacks under all-white systems that were set up decades, even centuries, ago when the city was all white; to bring "American know-how" to the newest technologies and emerging countries, meaning: to exploit them for profit when such exploitation can mean physical ruin and/or moral, physical degradation for literally millions; to prepare young people for a life which will never exist for them; to engage the world's finest scientific minds in the construction of hideous death machinery that is obsolete before finished. How can artists or any other thinking people cope with such monumental blindness in high places? Where does communication start? The "avant-garde," a convenient catch-phrase to blanket a colorful group of young *enfants terribles*. Perhaps once this would do. But no more!

We live in times which are much too dangerous for any such simple-minded, patronizing, amiable tolerance of those who are concerned with the future and are in a position to make concrete contributions toward a reasonably sane one. For these artists are not "ahead" of everyone else. They are exactly with their own stage of civilization, or, better, evolution. They are not creating art that is "ahead of its time" (that is an absurd notion); they create today's art, and it makes profound statements about today with clear implications about tomorrow. We are in the midst of the second industrial revolution, a new age of electricity, automation and constant change. Change is, and will continue to be, rapid, that is to say, violent, and necessarily breeds even more violence when institutions either cannot keep up or refuse to recognize the changes. And it comes to this: either the institutions keep up (in this context, heed the artists) or we all perish slowly or quickly.

But let's get down to business and try to determine, at least, for now, on the surface, what all this destructive art is about. Several rather simple and perhaps obvious comments can be made immediately. One may say that destroying a violin by fire or smashing it on a table represents a positive statement which may or may not be clear from the foregoing. First it is, to me at least, a very beautiful comment, with what would have to be described as an ultra-miniaturized subtleness, on the destructive, aggressive and schizophrenic nature of our ways, a sort of capsulated atomic bomb. Secondly, perhaps a little less crude and quite subtle in its own way, it suggests that the violin virtuoso is quite definitely out of a job, and that the institutions might then take note of a certain change in this situation along with, perhaps, the veritable host of implications contained in and radiating from this fact. But of course the real point of the matter is a purely musical one: this is one way to play the violin. Of course, the artist always seems to wish to speak to his colleagues; in this case he shows them all yet another way to play the fiddle, a very much appreciated point. The less subtle, less musical, points are there for the rest of us.

Subtle? Artistic? I think as subtle and as artistic as any music ever composed. How else might the artist communicate these insights? By writing a book? Could the artist drop a bomb? Climb a pole? Write an article on "New Ways to Play the Violin" and submit it to the music journals?

But all these interpretations and commentaries are first of all only barely touching the surface of the matter, and, secondly, are much too crass, too devoid of the genuine subtlety required in an analysis of any aspect of our exquisitely sophisticated civilization. Let us really look into the matter, calmly, dispassionately, and intellectually!

Ortega y Gasset pinpointed the problem some twenty years ago. What is it, he asked at that time, that makes artists turn against and savagely attack all past art? "Hatred of art," he said, "is unlikely to develop as an isolated phenomenon; it goes hand in hand with hatred of science, hatred of state, hatred, in sum, of civilization as a whole."[1]

Aha! There it is! Hatred of civilization as a whole. It's this that the artist tries to tell us about. And not hatred (necessarily, or especially) of his (my) own civilization, or that of Russia, etc., etc., but of civilization in general and Western civilization in particular. Hatred of civilization itself, the whole civilized business! But what is this civilized state but the very way that all of us civilized beings understand, interpret, and interact (collectively) with the world we live in? Civilization is what we have made it. It is the embodiment of the ways we think, of our very consciousness itself, our way of knowing and what we know. Hatred of art is hatred of civilization is hatred of self.

Listen! Listen!

Listen to the artist, to three (or four) artists who have seen further than most civilized men have been able to see, artists who have seen even into the promised land. To be sure they paid the price for their vision; they were too early and too few. But their time is come; too late for them, but scarcely for the rest of us. Look! Look at our civilization as the artist sees it, be it in London, Campfer, Paris, New York or Dallas, Texas.

1. Jose Ortega y Gasset, *The Dehumanization of Art* (Garden City, N.Y.: Doubleday & Company, 1956), p. 142.

> I wander thro' each charter'd street,
> Near where the charter'd Thames
>   does flow,
> And mark in every face I meet
> Marks of weakness, marks of woe.
>
> In every cry of every Man,
> In every Infant's cry of fear,
> In every voice, in every ban,
> The mind-forg'd manacles I hear.[2]

The mind-forg'd manacles = the Spectre = the ratio of things = Urizen (your reason) = man's highly reasoned way of seeing everything for use and profit in a utilitarian, mechanical, dehumanized world separated seemingly irrevocably, irretrievably, from a world of joy and richness, of profound feeling, of a welling union with the world of others. All separated, alienated "spirits" or ghostly goblins. That is what we are; that is what we have become.

And Vaslav Nijinsky saw exactly the same way that Blake saw. His own term for the mind-forg'd manacles, the ratio of things, was simply "thinking." We "think" too much; we have lost touch (as he, Nijinsky, or any other artist has not) with the world before "thinking," the world of truth, of the child in us all. Being "in touch" with the humanity within, with reality, poetically, religiously, aesthetically at one with mankind, with its basic oneness and goodness and richness; being thus fully in touch with one's unconscious, Nijinsky names, again very simply and beautifully: "feeling." Nijinsky feels great compassion for mankind caught ineluctably with the slimmest hope of salvation, in the mind-forg'd manacles of his very own manufacture. Mankind thinks too much, Nijinsky tells us, he feels too little. Of course, and most touchingly, his own wife is part of the mankind doomed to a living death, though not yet, as we shall see, his little daughter, Kyra.

Nijinsky:

2. William Blake, *The Portable Blake*, ed. Alfred Kazin (New York: The Viking Press, 1946), p. 112 ("London").

My wife thinks a lot but feels little, and [she] started to weep, so
that my throat swelled with tears and I wept, covering my face with
my hands. I was not ashamed but felt sad and was afraid for my
wife. Wishing her good, I did not know what to do. The whole life
of my wife and of all mankind is death.[3]

The joys of the world of feeling, the joys of eternity, the joys
only the child knows, and the saint, are filtered out, trapped in
our nets of reason, our institutions, our own traps, says Blake.
Blake:

> These were the Churches, Hospitals, Castles, Palaces,
> Like nets & gins & traps to catch the joys of Eternity.
>   And all the rest a desert;
> Till, like a dream, Eternity was obliterated & erased.[4]

Death for both these artists is never the death that the Christian knows but the death of a humanity that refuses to realize
its own humanity, a humanity trapped in its own meshes of
thought and the ensuing laws and institutions, the ensuing flight
from death which paradoxically is always a flight from life. But
the spectre, whether he be the Devil of mechanical, alienated
man or Urizen himself, need not exist, says Blake. Both he and
Nijinsky know that death is of this world and it is of the man who
refuses life and actually pursues death relentlessly. Yet it's not his
fault, or, at least, it need not be:
Nijinsky:

> Passing the hotel, I felt tears, understanding that the whole life in
> places like this is like death. Mankind makes merry and God
> mourns. It is not the fault of mankind.[5]

And now will Nijinsky's incredibly pure, shimmeringly, indelibly
straight-arrowed child-hearted attack on (with) one psychoanalytic truth (see Norman O. Brown) strike us as naïve any
more? A shudder or perhaps a whimper can be our only thinking
response to naïveté that we now know to be so devastatingly true:

3. Vaslav Nijinsky, *The Diary of Vaslav Nijinsky*, ed. Romda Nijinsky
(Berkeley: University of California Press, 1936), p. 38.
4. Blake, *op. cit.*, p. 365 ("The Song of Los: Africa").
5. Nijinsky, *op. cit.*

Nijinsky:

I want to have millions in order to make the Stock Exchange tremble. I want to ruin the Stock Exchange. I am life and life is love of people for one another. The Stock Exchange is death.[6]

And the knots tighten:
Blake:

> Then the thunders of Urizen
>   bellow'd aloud
> From his woven darkness above.[7]

> So twisted the cords, & so knotted
> The meshes. . . .

>   . . . a web, dark & cold
> the dark net of infection. . . .

> Till the shrunken eyes, clouded over,
> Discerned not the woven hipocrisy. . . .[8]

Antonin Artaud
        (on Van Gogh)
        "The Man Suicided by Society"
            (translated by
                Mary Beach
                + Lawrence Ferlinghetti)
M. Artaud: "It isn't man but the world has become abnormal,"[9] meaning that the matter has gotten beyond man's control unless he (man) can change himself, become more human, transform (resurrect) his body. Only then can a sick society be made well—by a transformed mankind. But,
    Artaud:

Things are bad because the sick conscience now has a vital interest in not getting over its sickness.

6. *Ibid.* p. 7.
7. Blake, p. 368 ("The Song of Los: Asia").
8. Blake, pp. 345–346 ("The First Book of Urizen," IX: 1, 2).
9. Antonin Artaud, *Anthology*, ed. Jack Hirschman, 2d ed., rev. (San Francisco: City Lights Books, 1965), p. 135.

So a sick society invented psychiatry to defend itself against the investigations of certain visionaries whose faculties of divination disturbed it.[10]

And Society Suicided Van Gogh

Question:

If every single person in the United States of America—except for President Nixon—got up every single morning and smashed a violin in the breakfast nook, how long would it be before the good president would be removed from office?

What is the psychopathology of the average? Is there something better?

Where do you fit in?

The man who "thinks" without "feeling" is schizophrenic. Such a consciousness belongs to one who has succeeded in splitting off thought from affect. But we all suffer this way; as Erich Fromm and some others have pointed out, we share our sickness with millions of others. Yet we look on ourselves as normal "and at those who have not lost the link between heart and mind as 'crazy.' In all low-grade forms of psychosis," Fromm tells us, "the definition of sickness depends on the question as to whether the pathology is shared or not."[11]

Caught in the jaws of the spectre, our situation is, as it now stands, hopeless. Yet most of us, even those who at least recognize in some measure the hopelessness, simply try to ignore it by adjusting to the majority. As Fromm puts it: "As long as everybody else whistles, [we] whistle too, and instead of feeling [our] hoplessness, [we] seem to participate in a kind of pop concert."[12]

Yet It Need Not Be

As Blake taught, there is no reason that man should limit himself as he does; he is free to wake up if only he will, in Nijinsky's

10. *Ibid.*
11. Erich Fromm, *The Revolution of Hope: Toward a Humanized Technology* (New York: Bantam Books, 1968) , p. 47.
12. *Ibid.*, p. 20.

terms again, feel rather than think, or rather, feel first and think second. He can change, and the results will not be predictable.

Blake:

> Each man is in his spectre's power
> Until the arrival of that hour
> When his humanity awakes
> And casts his spectre into the lake. . . .[13]

Blake, Nijinsky, and Artaud believed passionately that mankind could awake, that he could change his vision from that of the "Marks of weakness, marks of woe" to the vision of the artist, to a humanity capable not merely of thinking but of feeling, a humanity of artists, of seers, of children who are also fully mature, of a Great Humanity Divine. But no one dreamt that such a radical change of man could be anything less than cataclysmic.

Artaud:

> So the question here is revolution,
> and everyone is crying out for a necessary
> revolution, but I don't know if enough
> people have understood that this revolution
> would not be real as long as it was
> not physically and materially complete,
> as long as it would not turn and face man,
> face the body of man himself
> and decide once and for all to demand
> that *he change*.[14]

Can we change? We must (the question only is how). We will. We already are changing to a significant extent. A beginning has been made. Men have begun to see the unbearable, inhuman burden of the machinery, the systems that they have built and unwittingly, stupidly come to idolize. The systems can be overcome, are easily overcome, on the artistic level, through chance and other techniques. And the negation of man-made systems, in art as anywhere, does not result in vacuous inanity but in a renewed

13. [Quoted in] Colin Wilson, *The Outsider* (New York: Dell Publishing Co., 1956) , p. 238.
14. Artaud, p. 170 ("Theatre and Science," trans. by Daniel Moore) .

ability to see something like what Van Gogh and Nijinsky, Artaud and Blake, could see: a world that is beautiful and joyous in and of itself. Man has already learned, at least on the artistic level, how to cast his spectre into the lake and to see the world aright.

Blake could pinpoint the problem. He knew that the kernel of Western man's looming alienation from himself and his humanity was in his blinkered, woven, twisted, reasoning, narrowing, strangling form of consciousness. But he could only attempt to chart the area with a mythology of alienation. Van Gogh could see both ways: now as all sleepers see *(The Potato Eaters)* or again as the visionary, the poet, the prophet, the child *(Cypresses by Moonlight)*. But he died with words of a Potato Eater: "Misery will never End."[15] Nijinsky and Artaud were suicided by society so quickly and thoroughly that they really only could begin to articulate, verbally, the horrendous problem of mankind, the real problem set the artist. They never had the opportunity to meet and try to solve this problem on the artistic level.

Only in mid-twentieth century has the artist learned, on the artistic level, to break the systems that bind him, to cast off the mind-forg'd manacles. In the works of artists like LaMonte Young, John Cage, Terry Riley, George Brecht, Robert Rauschenberg, Robert Ashley, the happening people, the inter-medias, the Judson performers, some of the Rock-Light show people, Willis Ward, Jackson Pollock, James Fulkerson, Merce Cunningham, Ornette Coleman, the late John Coltrane, the jazz-light-show experimental church services of Glide Memorial Methodist Church in San Francisco, Erik Hawkins, Lucia Dlugoszewski and others the systems of Western art (the mirror of Western consciousness, the embodiment of Western Civilization) have been, however briefly, cast into the lake, smashed, revealing an incredibly rich and fascinating, perfectly, purely, wonderingly marvelous field of possibilty. And the possibility is of more life, of a changed, transformed, renewed Western man, a new man who can face the East, as himself, as a whole man. It is only a matter of bringing, somehow, this art into our lives, of being transformed *permanently* by it.

15. [Quoted in] Wilson, *op. cit.*, p. 106.

On the artistic level Western man has awakened. Everything is before him. Everything is to be done. He is free!

Destruction. Yes, destruction. But this destruction that artists like Blake through Nijinsky and Artaud knew somehow had to take place, the destruction which the American avant-garde has come to visit on us, is a merciful destruction which is no destruction at all but a liberation.

Man need *not* live out his life in the prisons that he himself has made. He need *not* worship as idols the work of his own hands, the very civilization and technocracy—even his great art, his God—that he himself constructed in the image of his own consciousness and which now threatens either to strangle him or to obliterate him. Things are, as Emerson said, in the saddle and ride mankind, *but it need not be.*

The artists ask man to change, indeed they demand it. They ask him to transform himself, to grow up, to wake up, *wachet auf!* in order that he himself then may transform his own institutions, the civilization that he made in the image of a now inadequate consciousness, that he may make it over into another image, in the image of another consciousness, another and more adequate vision of himself, his powers, his love, his humanity.

We must change. We must wake up. And we can change. We can wake up. We can cast our spectre into the lake. We can learn to feel, to know, to see, and to love. We have sold ourselves short; we are capable of so much!

The nets, the meshes, the webs, dark and cold, webs and meshes that lead ineluctably to deadly cold steel and the infernal acids of hate and napalm, are of our own making. The society (the form of consciousness) that suicided Van Gogh and is intent on suiciding itself—after Vietnam—all these are of our own making.

The nets, the meshes, the webs are imbedded in our arts even as they make up our consciousness. It is to the destruction of this false consciousness that the destruction of art can and must help lead. What remains after this destruction is all humanity, all the humanity that in the West has been, for so many of us, lost—if only the merciful destruction of civilization through art (or any other means) can wake us to this humanity within us and uniting us, before the actual and virtual destruction can take place.

Van Gogh was suicided by society. So, really, was Nijinsky. So was Artaud. They had awakened. (Blake survived pretty much as a bitter recluse.) These were the awakened ones amongst the sleeping millions. *They had to be eliminated.*

But to be an awakened one, it is not necessary also to be a great artist. All that is needed is the ability to feel, in addition to the ability to think, *and to put this first.* All that is needed is the ability to live in the real world of human warmth and aliveness instead of the symbolic, conceptual world of words and paper currency and I.B.M. cards. And, since Blake, the awakened ones have been growing in great numbers in our society, in Europe and in America, all, it seems, very young. Their number is already so great that society simply cannot suicide them all, though parts of society will try. That same society faces with an incredibly stupid hostility literally billions in Asia and Africa and more millions at home who, because they derive from older cultures or because they are among the awakened ones, see things (feel things), in many ways, just as Nijinsky and Artaud, Van Gogh and Blake saw them.

The consciousness that built Western civilization is obsolete and a threat to the world. It must be changed, remolded, "dis-alienated." If this entails, among other things, the destruction of the art we have known, then the artist must destroy in order to affirm.

It is only the second function of art to pass on the transcript of the past, to inculcate, to reinforce the consciousness that we inherit (though our institutions, criminally I think, confine themselves almost exclusively to this second function). The first function of art is to enlarge that consciousness, to transform it, to prepare it to deal with the realities of the world with which it *now* interacts and which it will be called on to contemplate and interact with in the future. The latter necessarily entails that the former be overcome.

To those who can believe that they can change the world without first changing themselves there is nothing to be said.

Every day we choose between living under the spectre and seeing the world aright. Perhaps we are forever doomed to wobble between the two, like poor Van Gogh.

But we must decide which of the two is to rule us. At each

moment we must and do decide between Van Gogh's last words, "Misery will never end," and Nijinsky's response to the very great child-knowledge of his little girl, Kyra (children, knowing only eternity, never wobble):

Nijinsky:

My little girl is singing: "Ah, ah, ah, ah!" I do not understand its meaning, but I feel what she wants to say. She wants to say that everything—Ah! Ah!—is not horror but joy.[16]

16. Nijinsky, *op. cit.*, p. 184.